Idelisse Malavé is an organizational consultant who ran the Tides Foundation in California for eleven years and was vice president of the Ms. Foundation. She co-authored, with Elizabeth Debold and Marie Wilson, *Mother Daughter Revolution*. Born in Puerto Rico, she grew up and lives in New York City.

Esti Giordani, a New York–born Puerto Rican, is a writer living in Los Angeles. She currently works in television. Until recently, she was a communications strategist and blogger for the Social Transformation Project.

Also by Idelisse Malavé

Mother Daughter Revolution
(with Elizabeth Debold and Marie Wilson)

LATINO STATS

American Hispanics by the Numbers

IDELISSE MALAVÉ
ESTI GIORDANI

THE NEW PRESS

NEW YORK
LONDON

© 2015 by Idelisse Malavé and Esti Giordani

Requests for permission to reproduce selections from this book should be mailed to: Permissions Department, The New Press, 120 Wall Street, 31st floor, New York, NY 10005.

Published in the United States by The New Press, New York, 2015
Distributed by Perseus Distribution

978-1-59558-961-3 (pbk.)
978-1-62097-019-5 (e-book)
CIP data is available

The New Press publishes books that promote and enrich public discussion and understanding of the issues vital to our democracy and to a more equitable world. These books are made possible by the enthusiasm of our readers; the support of a committed group of donors, large and small; the collaboration of our many partners in the independent media and the not-for-profit sector; booksellers, who often hand-sell New Press books; librarians; and above all by our authors.

www.thenewpress.com

Book design and composition by Bookbright Media
This book was set in Avenir LT and Jockey

Printed in the United States of America

10 9 8 7 6 5 4 3 2 1

This book is dedicated to Alberto "Tata" Malavé and Emma "Nani" Carattini. Like so many others, you traveled far and crossed borders to get here. Thank you for all you did to help us flourish.

CONTENTS

Thanks first to researcher par excellence, Erin Meggyessy, for all your help along the way. You were an indispensable addition to this project. Many thanks to Amanda Verwey, Gabriel Giordani, Jodie Tonita, Sandra García Betancourt, the women of *That Creative Thing*, Essence Harden, Lauren Shell, Paul Sheffield, Owen Morse, Gabriel Kenny, Sophie Hinrichsen, Ramona Gonzalez, Ali Liebegott, and Emma Carattini for your loving support throughout the writing of this book.

ACKNOWLEDGMENTS

Even well-educated, amiable, open-minded
people in the United States do not realize
that their country has a Hispanic past, as well
as a Hispanic future.

—*Felipe Fernandea-Armesto*
Our America: A Hispanic History of the
United States

The growing Latino presence in the United States
matters, and most of us, non-Latino and Latino alike,
are just beginning to pay attention to what it means
for all of us. The sheer number of Latinos living in the
United States today is more likely to have grabbed our
attention than Latinos' crucial role in America's unfold-
ing future. The numbers *are* staggering. Right now,
with 53 million Latinos in the United States, one in six
Americans is Latino. In three short decades, it will be
closer to one in three.

Latinos are not a homogenous group. American
Latinos—also frequently referred to as *Hispanics*—are
a *pan-ethnic* group with roots in nineteen Spanish-
speaking Latin American countries and Spain. The majority of Latinos living in the United States today were
born here, but a third are immigrants, and many more
are the children and grandchildren of immigrants. Most
speak English well, but also speak Spanish. Some don't
speak English, and others don't speak Spanish. Racially
diverse, many Latinos acknowledge a mixed-race heritage that often varies by country of origin. Latinos are
a much younger population than Whites or African
Americans, but some national origin groups in the
mix are years older or younger than the average for
all Latinos. As a group, they are characterized by economic, political, social, and cultural differences, as well
as similarities. Some Latinos have roots in this country
that reach further back than any other racial or ethnic

group in the country except for Native Americans. Ignored by history books and the media, Latino history in the United States extends far beyond the current immigration debate.

Before the English established their first settlement in the New World, Spanish *conquistadores* probed forty-eight of the fifty states. With more than five hundred years of history in North America, Spaniards and Mexicans were already in lands annexed by the United States in the nineteenth century through wars and treaties fueled by American "Manifest Destiny" that increased the size of the United States by one-third, including all or parts of ten states. Puerto Rico, still a territory of the United States today, was acquired at the end of the Spanish American War of 1898.

While Spaniards and Mexicans have an especially long history in the United States, waves of immigration from across Latin America from the 1930s to the 1980s doubled Latino representation in the United States in a fifty-year period. Today, Mexicans are still the largest Latino group in our country and our largest immigrant group.

Although the United States is routinely and proudly referred to as "a country of immigrants," waves of immigration still inspire economic and cultural fears. Latino immigrants have been greeted with a familiar litany, most commonly, "They're stealing our jobs!" In the 1930s that fear, captured by a Hoover administration slogan, "American jobs for real Americans," led to federal and local authorities forcibly deporting an estimated 1 million Mexicans living in the United States, including a shocking six hundred thousand U.S. citizens, without due process. Often randomly picked up off the streets and loaded onto buses, Mexican Americans were taken to Mexico and stranded there. In 2006 the State of California adopted "The Apology Act," acknowledging its role in what is euphemistically known as the *Mexican Repatriation*. The federal government has yet to apologize.

The economic fears that shaped these events are still present today but changing. The focus of the immigrant debate has shifted to undocumented immigrants, most of whom are Mexicans and other Latinos. In the past, undocumented immigration was less of an issue simply because the United States placed fewer restrictions on immigration than it does now. The ongoing economic crisis intensified fears that undocumented immigrants are "stealing jobs." Yet the majority of Americans in this country are not giving into those fears. Instead, seven-in-ten Republicans and eight-in-ten Democrats believe that "[m]ost undocumented immigrants are hard workers who should have the opportunity to stay in this country and improve their lives." Perhaps the average American is coming to understand that American economic woes cannot be blamed on immigrants, that instead, as most economists agree, immigrant workers grow the economy as well as the demand for goods and services that creates jobs.

The cultural fears that usually accompany these economic fears center on assimilation or acculturation. Often-quoted Harvard historian Samuel Huntington named Latin American immigrants, especially Mexicans, as *the single most immediate and most serious challenge to America's traditional identity.* Underlying his alarm is the idea that America is a "melting pot," an idea that is giving way to a view of our country as more of a "mosaic" or "salad bowl." Trepidations about the loss of a traditional national identity often focus first on language, yet most Latinos in the United States speak English well. Many of them also speak Spanish and want their children and grandchildren to be bilingual as well. And oddly, values usually attributed to Latinos are solidly in line with traditional American values, mainly love of and loyalty to family and a strong work ethic. Latinos subscribe to the American Dream, a belief that hard work leads to success, at higher rates than the general public.

Why then are there fears that Latinos don't or won't assimilate? Two primary reasons come to mind. The first is one alluded to earlier, namely, a view of identity as static and exclusive rather than evolving. Most Latinos are integrating into an *American* culture, but they also want to hold on to valued parts of their own heritage, to be part of the diverse American mosaic. Latinos are also influencing American culture. *Salsa*, both the music and the condiment, has certainly crossed over into mainstream culture. Salsa outsells ketchup, and more Americans are buying tortillas than hamburger or hot-dog buns. The majority of Americans appreciate Latino influences on American food and music tastes; they also recognize Latinos' political influence. That influence doesn't impact just election outcomes. It also shapes views on the environment and social issues. While only half of the general American public believes that climate change is happening, three-quarters of Latinos do. An equal share of Latinos also believes that the women's movement supports not just women's needs, but those of men and children. At the same time Latinos are more conservative on the abortion issue but are as equally supportive of gay rights as other Americans.

The second reason for concerns about Latinos' impact on "America's traditional identity" has to do with racism. Latinos, especially Mexicans, sometimes refer to themselves as *La Raza* ("the Race"). This expression is a shortened form of *La Raza Cósmica* ("the Cosmic Race"), a term coined by Mexican philosopher José Vasconcelos in the early part of the twentieth century. *La Raza* lifts up and values the racially mixed population of Latin Americans, a combination of indigenous peoples, Europeans, Africans, and Asians. This view collides with the more stratified, Black-or-White construction of race in the United States. It also helps explain why 18.5 million Latinos checked the slippery "other" racial category in the 2010 U.S. Census. When given the opportunity, slightly more than half of Latinos identify as "some other race" or volunteer "Hispanic/Latino." Just 36 percent identify as White, and only 3 percent as Black. Many Latinos simply cannot fit themselves into existing U.S. racial categories. Conversely, other Americans—mired in the White-or-Black understanding of race—don't have a problem placing Latinos on the less privileged side of the racial divide.

Discrimination is a recognized reality for most Latinos. About two-thirds of Latinos believe that anti-Latino discrimination is a "major problem." Race, a key driver for structural, conscious, and unconscious bias, is made more potent by anti-immigrant and language discrimination. A quarter of the general public believes Latinos are targets of discrimination more often than any other racial or ethnic group in the country. Inequity and limited opportunity are the result.

Most Latinos live in segregated, low-income neighborhoods. Those who live in those neighborhoods tend to earn less money, often working low-paying, service-industry jobs. They have to travel further to get to work and rely on public transportation that just isn't as good as it is in other parts of their cities. Their children go to under-resourced, underperforming public schools, and they don't have easy access to good health care or healthy foods for their families. It is unlikely that the elected officials who represent them are Latinos, and casting their votes is often made harder by suppression tactics.

Alongside these sad realities are many hopeful ones. The Latino high school dropout rate has declined dramatically to 14 percent and is expected to continue to fall. In 2012, for the first time, more Latino high school graduates went on to enroll in college than White graduates. Annual income for all Latinos has been rising, marked by particularly sharp increases in the numbers of Latinos earning $50,000 or more. The poverty rate has decreased. Latinos continue to surprise public health experts by being healthier and hardier than anyone would expect given the challenges they face. As a rule, Latinos live years longer than Whites and African Americans. In just fifteen or so years, the number of Latino voters will double. With an influx of college-educated and wealthier young Latinos entering the electorate, current voter participation rates, lower than non-Latino rates, are expected to increase as well.

These general statements about Latinos are not meant to mask their differences, but to point to some commonalities among the majority of Latinos that cut across national origin. While most Latinos still describe themselves first by country of origin (Mexican, Puerto Rican, Salvadoran, etc.), a sense of "shared fate" links them. The pan-ethnic Latino is at least a complementary identity, and an important one. Nearly three-quarters of Latinos in the United States believe that their "success depends on the success of other Latinos/ Hispanics." As the data captured in this book show, Latino solidarity is already shaping the American political, economic, social, and cultural landscape.

ABOUT THE BOOK

We have sifted through a profusion of data to identify the most telling and often surprising facts of contemporary Latino life with glimpses of the past and future. We cover basic demographics, immigration, voting, education, entertainment, and more, to offer a broad sense of the Latino community. The data in the book are drawn primarily from federal and state government sources, private sector surveys, nonprofits, and reliable media sources. The information and sources we share also serve as a starting point to delve deeper.

Statistics are useful in describing groups, cataloguing inequities, and debunking misplaced preconceptions. They are also limited—numbers alone simply cannot capture all the nuances.

Throughout the book we use the term *Latino* rather than *Hispanic* to describe Americans with roots in twenty Spanish-speaking countries. It is a personal preference. Forty years ago, the federal government officially adopted the term *Hispanic* and then later *Latino* to be used interchangeably. While most Latinos identify first by country of origin, polls show that most are also comfortable with the use of either *Hispanic* or *Latino* and don't have a preference between the two.

We refer to the diverse Latino national origin groups living in the United States as *Mexicans, Puerto Ricans, Cubans, Dominicans, Salvadorans*, etc., and provide available and relevant comparative data. Non-Hispanic Blacks are described as *African American*, and non-Hispanic Whites as *Whites*, again providing available comparative data to highlight meaningful disparities.

Finally, because this is a book about Latinos, we thought it was important to say that we are both Puerto Rican. Idelisse was born in Puerto Rico, but raised in New York. She came to the United States as a small child and, while not counted an immigrant by the U.S. government, shares an immigrant experience with other Latino immigrants. Her daughter, Esti, a second generation Puerto Rican, was born in New York and was raised there and in California. We expect that our different generations, experiences, and perspectives as Latinas have served to enrich the research and writing of the book.

Esti Giordani
Idelisse Malavé

LATINO STATS

Demographic transformations are dramas told in slow motion. They unfold incrementally, almost imperceptibly, tick by tock, without trumpets or press conferences.

—*Paul Taylor*, The Next America: Boomers, Millennials and the Looming Generational Showdown

SNAP STATS

The Latino population is sizeable and growing. An estimated 53 million Latinos live in the United States today. Latinos are currently the second largest racial/ethnic group in the United States today, fewer than White Americans (around 198 million) and more numerous than African Americans (around 40 million).

By 2050 there will be a projected 112 million Latinos in the United States, representing the largest share of the "New Majority." * From 2000 to 2010 the Latino population increased by 15.2 million (a 43 percent jump) and accounted for more than half of total population growth in the United States in those ten years. The Latino population is expected to continue to grow at higher rates than the total population for decades to come.

Contrary to popular belief, the majority of Latinos were born in the United States. Two-thirds of the

---

*By 2050, minority populations (Latinos, African Americans, Asian Americans, etc.) combined will outnumber the aging White population thus forming the "New Majority."

Latino population were born here and the other third are immigrants. Three out of four of all Latinos are U.S. citizens.

The majority of Latinos in the United States are Mexican. Twenty Latino national origin groups are represented in the United States. Mexicans are the largest national origin group in the United States, with a population of 33.6 million, followed by the 4.9 million Puerto Ricans—a distant second.

Latinos are the youngest racial/ethnic group in the country. The average age of Latinos is twenty-seven years old, compared to forty-two years old for Whites and thirty-six for African Americans.

The majority of Latinos speak English very well. Almost 60 percent of Latino adults and 90 percent of Latino children are proficient in English. One-third of all Latinos are fully bilingual.

BY THE NUMBERS...

How many Latinos live in the United States?

- In 2010, 50.5 million Latinos lived in the United States.[1] In 2013, the U.S. Census Bureau estimated that the number of Latinos exceeded 53 million.[2]
- Of the 50.5 million Latinos in 2010, 25 million were women and 25.7 million were men.[3]
- One in every six Americans is Latino.[4]
- Latinos are the second largest racial/ethnic group in the United States, behind Whites and ahead of African Americans.[5]

Mexico is the only other country in the world with a larger Latino population than the United States.[6]

How quickly is the Latino population growing?

Latino population growth between 2000 and 2010 accounted for more than half of the United States' total population growth.[7]

- The Latino population increased by 15.2 million or 43 percent from 2000 to 2010. Of that increase 11.1 million were Mexican, 1.2 million were Puerto Rican, and 600,000 were Cuban.[8]
- The Latino population doubled between 2000 and 2010 in one out of four counties across the United States.[9]
- Latino population growth is now driven by the children and grandchildren of immigrants, as the population of Latino immigrants in the nation continues to decline.[10]
- By 2050, the total U.S. population is projected to grow to almost 400 million, of which 28 percent or about 112 million will be Latino. This is double the number today. [11]
- Projected population growth rates for Latinos in the coming decades range from 23 percent in 2015 (compared to 7 percent for the total population) to 13 percent in 2050 (compared to 5 percent for the total population).[12]

How many Latinos were born in the U.S?

- Two out of every three Latinos in the United States today were born here.[13]
- Latino immigrants born outside the United States make up 37 percent of the U.S. Latino population.[14]
- Each year one out of four babies born in the United States is born to a Latino mother.[15]

How many Latinos are U.S. citizens?

- Three-quarters of Latinos are U.S. citizens, close to 40 million people.[16]
- In 2012, almost 24 million Latino citizens were eligible

to vote. Of the total Latino population, 55 percent could not vote because they were not yet eighteen years old or were noncitizens.[17]

What are the major Latino national origin groups?

☐ Two-thirds or 33.6 million Latinos in the United States are of Mexican descent or origin.[18]

☐ Puerto Ricans are the second largest Latino group in the United States, with a population of over 4.9 million. Another 3.7 million live in Puerto Rico, a U.S.

Figure 1. U.S. Hispanic Population, by Origin, 2011
(in thousands)

All Hispanics   51,927

		% of Hispanics
Mexican	33,539	64.6
Puerto Rican	4,916	9.5
Salvadoran	1,952	3.8
Cuban	1,889	3.6
Dominican	1,528	2.9
Guatemalan	1,216	2.3
Colombian	989	1.9
Spaniard	707	1.4
Honduran	702	1.4
Ecuadorian	645	1.2
Peruvian	556	1.1
Nicaraguan	395	0.8
Venezuelan	259	0.5
Argentinean	242	0.5

Note: Total U.S. population is 311,592,000 (rounded to the nearest thousand). Tabulation based on U.S. Census Bureau's 2011 American Community Survey (ACS).

Source: Mark Hugo Lopez, Ana Gonzalez-Barrera, and Danielle Cuddington, "Diverse Origins: The Nation's 14 Largest Hispanic-Origin Groups," Pew Research Center, Hispanic Trends Project, June 19, 2013.

---

territory, but are not included in national population figures.[19]

- Over three-quarters of all Latinos in the United States in 2011 were Mexican, Puerto Rican, or Salvadoran.[20]
- Six Latino national origin groups have populations of one million or more in the United States.[21]

What languages do most Latinos speak?

- A majority (59 percent) of adult Latinos and nearly nine out of ten (86 percent) Latino children speak English very well.[22]
- Three-fourths of Latinos are proficient in Spanish.[23]
- One out of three Latinos is fully bilingual.[24]
- *Spanglish* is a mix of English and Spanish used in a sentence, conversation, or writing (e.g., "Hasta la vista, baby!"). Although common among Latinos of all ages, Spanglish usage data is available only for Latino youth sixteen to twenty-five years old. Nearly a quarter of Latino youth use Spanglish most of the time and nearly another half use it some of the time.[25]
- Puerto Ricans (82 percent), Mexicans (64 percent), Colombians (59 percent), and Peruvians (59 percent) have the highest English proficiency rates among Latino national origin groups.[26]
- One out of three Latinos is Spanish dominant, while more than half of U.S.-born Latinos are English dominant.[27]
- 25 percent of Latinos five years of age and older speak only English at home, while 74 percent speak Spanish at home (this includes those who are proficient in English and may speak some English at home).[28]
- The vast majority of Latinos, close to 90 percent, believe that learning English is important.[29]

What is the age breakdown of Latinos?

- Latinos are the youngest major ethnic or racial group

in the country: the average age of Latinos is twenty-seven, compared to forty-two for Whites, thirty-three for African Americans, and thirty-six for Asians.[30]

◻ The youngest Latino groups are Mexicans (twenty-five), Puerto Ricans (twenty-seven), and Guatemalans (twenty-seven). Cubans are the oldest Latino group with a median age of forty.[31]

◻ Over 20 percent of Latinos are millennials, ages twenty to thirty-four.[32]

Every day over 2,200 Latinos turn eighteen years of age—one every forty seconds or so.[33]

◻ Only 5 percent of Latinos were sixty-five years old or older in 2010, compared to over 16 percent of Whites.[34]

Where do Latinos live in the United States?

Two-thirds of Latinos live in just five states: California (14.4 million), Texas (9.8 million), Florida (4.4 million), New York (3.5 million), and Illinois (2.1 million).[35]

◻ Five other states, however, have experienced the fastest Latino population growth since 2000: Alabama, South Carolina, Tennessee, Kentucky, and South Dakota.[36]

◻ Latinos were projected to outnumber Whites in California by 2014.[37]

◻ Regionally, Latinos represent almost 30 percent of the total population in the West, 16 percent in the South, 13 percent in the Northeast, and 7 percent in the Midwest.[38]

◻ Three out of four Latinos live in the West (41 percent) and South (36 percent), while 14 percent of Latinos live in the Northeast and 9 percent in the Midwest.[39]

What is the racial makeup of Latinos?

- Accommodating U.S. racial definitions can be difficult for Latinos, as seen in their responses to the 2010 U.S. Census list of racial identities. Of the responses,18.5 million Latinos (37 percent) chose "Other," and another three million (6 percent) chose "Two or more races."[40]

- A total of 53 percent of Latinos identified their race as White, 2 percent as Black, and 0.7 percent as indigenous in the Census.[41]

- However, in a 2012 survey conducted by the Pew Research Center, a total of 51 percent of Latinos either identified as "some other race" (26 percent) or volunteered "Hispanic/Latino" as their race (25 percent). Just 36 percent identified as White and 3 percent as Black.[42]

We come to work, we come for a better life, we come to participate in the American Dream.

—*Antonio Villaraigosa, former Mayor of Los Angeles*

The 500-year Latino presence in the United States is surpassed only by Native Americans. Latinos came here via many different avenues: as Spanish *conquistadores* and colonizers, well before other Europeans; through wars and treaties that left Mexicans and Spaniards on the other side of changed borders; through the trans-Atlantic slave trade; and as immigrants and refugees in search of a better life. Today, the majority of Latinos living in the United States are the children and grandchildren of immigrants, while just a third are immigrants themselves. Struggling for opportunity, they face and are overcoming many obstacles to building the "better life" that led them here. And our country needs them. Often cast as the source of our economic woes, immigrants add billions of dollars to the American economy and are crucial to maintaining our labor force. The White population is aging, and over time the population of older Americans will depend on a labor force of younger workers that would shrink dangerously without an influx of immigrants. The economic incentive alone serves as a strong rationale for reforming our immigration policies.

SNAP STATS

Latinos are the largest immigrant group in the United States today. Nearly half of the 40 million immigrants in the United States come from nineteen Spanish-speaking Latin American countries and Spain.

While many Latinos—one in three—are immigrants, the majority are not.

Net migration from Mexico fell to zero in 2011, with return migration to Mexico equaling new arrivals to the United States. Immigrants from Mexico are the largest national origin immigrant group in the country. While the Mexican migration rate has fallen these last few years, the total U.S. immigrant population continues to grow.

Only 17 percent of all Latinos are undocumented immigrants. While a majority of Americans mistakenly believe the number of undocumented immigrants in the country is growing, it actually has been declining since 2007.

During the Obama administration, a record-breaking four hundred thousand immigrants a year have been deported at a cost of billions of dollars. That is a 30 percent increase over the past Bush administration.

Almost three-fourths of the 18.7 million Latino immigrants work and pay taxes. That includes undocumented immigrants who pay over $10 billion annually in state taxes alone even though they do not have access to any of the important government benefits that citizens and permanent residents enjoy.

BY THE NUMBERS . . .

How many Latinos are immigrants?

- Contrary to popular belief, the majority of Latinos in the United States are not immigrants.[1]
- Of the 51.9 million Latinos living in the fifty states in 2011, 33 million, almost two out of three, were born in the United States and its territories, including Puerto Rico.[2]

- Only 18.7 million were born outside of the United States and its territories.[3]
- Puerto Ricans who immigrate to the fifty states from the island are not counted as immigrants by the U.S. Census Bureau. Less than one third of Puerto Ricans living in the fifty states, or 1.5 million, were born on the island.[4]
- Men make up 52 percent of Latino immigrants and 48 percent are women.[5] Mexican immigrants have the highest proportion of men (54 percent), while South American and Caribbean immigrants have the lowest proportion of men (46 percent).[6]
- Latinos are the nation's largest immigrant group. Of the 40 million immigrants in the United States, nearly half (47 percent) are Latinos.[7]

Are there significant changes in Latino migration rates and trends?

- The percentage of Latinos who are immigrants declined from 40 percent in 2000 to 36 percent in 2010. This decline is due to an increase in Latinos born in the United States rather than a decrease in the number of immigrants.[8]
- The overall Latino immigrant population in the United States continues to grow steadily, while unauthorized immigration slows.[9]

The net migration rate from Mexico has fallen to zero, with return migration to Mexico equaling new arrival rates to the United States.[10]

What are the different countries of origin for Latino immigrants?

- Mexico yields 29 percent of the Latino immigrants in the United States, while 9 percent are from the Caribbean, 8 percent are from the rest of Central America, and 7 percent are from South America.[11]
- An estimated 11.7 million U.S. immigrants are from Mexico, making them the single largest national

Figure 2.1. Latino Immigrant Population by Country of Origin

	Number
Mexico	1,691,632
El Salvador	1,245,458
Cuba	1,090,563
Dominican Republic	878,858
Guatemala	844,332
Colombia	655,096
Honduras	499,987
Ecuador	429,316
Peru	406,008
Nicaragua	249,037
Venezuela	198,468
Argentina	165,027
Chile	99,430
Spain	93,578
Costa Rica	76,193
Uruguay	43,811

Source: Seth Motel and Eileen Patten, "Statistical Portrait of the Foreign-Born Population in the United States, 2011," Pew Research Center, Hispanic Trends Project, January 19, 2013.

origin immigrant group in the country.[12] (The second largest national origin group among all immigrants is Chinese.)[13]

- The percentage of immigrants versus U.S. native-born Latinos has decreased for all national origin groups since 2000.[14]
- The majority of Puerto Ricans (69 percent) and Mexicans (65 percent) living in the United States were born in the fifty states or the District of Columbia. The majority of all other Latino national origin populations are foreign born.[15]

Why do Latinos migrate to the United States?

- More than half of Latino immigrants (55 percent) name economic opportunities as their reason for coming to the United States.[16]
- Another 24 percent of Latino immigrants cite "family reasons."[17]
- Just 9 percent came to "pursue educational opportunities."[18]
- Eight out of ten Latino immigrants say that if they had it to do it again, they would.[19]

A solid majority of Latino immigrants believes that the United States offers more opportunities to get ahead (87 percent), is better for raising children (72 percent), and treats the poor better (69 percent).[20]

How many Latinos are U.S. citizens?

Three out of four of all Latinos in the United States are citizens.[21]

- 32 percent of Latino immigrants are naturalized citizens.[22]
- Only 49 percent of eligible Latino immigrants become citizens, compared to 72 percent of the immigrants from other parts of the world. Among Mexican immigrants, the naturalization rate is even lower (36 percent).[23]
- All Puerto Ricans, whether born in the fifty states or in the U.S. territory of Puerto Rico, are U.S. citizens by birth.[24]
- In a recent survey, more than nine in ten (93 percent) Latino immigrants who were eligible to apply for citizenship but haven't yet, said they would "if they could." They cited costs and administrative barriers,

English proficiency, and personal reasons (such as fears of the citizenship test) for not doing so.[25]

▢ Nine out of ten undocumented immigrants say they would become citizens if they could.[26]

Figure 2.2. Percentage of Latino Citizens By National Origin

Puerto Rican	93%
Cuban	74%
Mexican	74%
Nicaraguan	72%
Dominican	71%
Argentinian	68%
Colombian	68%
Peruvian	65%
Ecuadorian	64%
Salvadoran	58%
Venezuelan	55%
Guatemalan	51%
Honduran	50%

Source: Mark Hugo Lopez, Ana Gonzalez-Barrera, and Danielle Cuddington, "Diverse Origins: The Nation's 14 Largest Hispanic-Origin Groups," Pew Research Center, Hispanic Trends Project, June 19, 2013.

How many Latino immigrants have a "green card" (i.e., are authorized permanent residents of the United States)?

▢ Out of 18.7 million Latino immigrants in 2011, 5.4 million were permanent residents eligible for naturalization.[27]

▢ Other immigrants are citizens, hold temporary visas and others are undocumented.

How many Latinos are undocumented immigrants?

▢ Of the 11.7 million undocumented immigrants in the United States in 2012, 52 percent were Mexican. The U.S. Department of Homeland Security estimated that in 2011 about 80 percent of all undocumented immigrants were Latino.[28]

□ Just 17 percent of all Latinos are undocumented immigrants.[29]

□ About one out of five (22 percent) of all Latinos 16 to 25 years old are undocumented immigrants.[30]

Total numbers of unauthorized immigrants in the United States declined sharply from 12.2 million in 2007 to current estimates of 11.7 million. Nonetheless, a majority of the American public still believes it is increasing.[31]

□ Much of this decline is due to the shrinking numbers of unauthorized Mexican immigrants in the United States. That decline, from 6.7 million in 2007 to 6 million in 2012, is due both to a reduction in new arrivals and a marked increase in return migration to Mexico.[32]

Are many Latino immigrants deported?

□ Most Americans are unaware that from 1929 to 1939, with a public tagline of "American jobs for real Americans," an estimated 1 million Mexicans living in the United States, including a shocking 600,000 U.S. citizens of Latino descent, were forcibly deported without due process by federal and local authorities. Under federal law, U.S. citizens cannot be deported.[33]

During the Obama administration, deportations reached a record level of 400 thousand non-citizens per year, a 30 percent increase over deportation levels in George W. Bush's second term.[34]

□ Latinos are disproportionately deported. Although they represented 81 percent of the unauthorized immigrant population in 2010, 97 percent of all deportees were Latino.[35]

□ Mexican immigrants alone accounted for nearly three-fourths (73 percent) of deportees. Another 24 percent were from other countries in Latin America, including Guatemala (8 percent), Honduras (6 percent), and El Salvador (5 percent).[36]

□ Each deportation costs U.S. taxpayers almost $24,000 to apprehend, detain, process, and transport a single person.[37] At that rate, the total cost for 400,000 deportations is $9.6 billion.

□ In a recent poll, one in four Latinos said they knew someone who was deported in the last year.[38]

How long have most Latino immigrants lived in the United States?

Two-thirds of Latino immigrants entered the United States before 2000 and have lived here for fourteen years or longer.[39]

□ 28 percent of Latino immigrants in the United States in 2010 arrived between 1990 and 1999.[40]

□ 20 percent of Latino immigrants entered the United States between 1980 and 1989. [41]

□ 17 percent of Latino immigrants arrived in the United States before 1980.[42]

How strong are Latino immigrants' ties to their home countries?

□ Two-thirds of Latino immigrants plan to stay in the United States for good.[43]

Two out of five Latino immigrants telephone friends and relatives at least once a week.[44]

□ 65 percent of Latino immigrants have traveled back to their native countries at least once since moving to the United States.[45]

> A majority (54 percent) of Latino immigrants send money to relatives in their home countries. In 2012 their remittances to Spanish-speaking Latin American countries totaled $41 billion.[46]

What states have the largest concentrations of Latino immigrants?

- ❏ Over 60 percent of Latino immigrants to the United States live in just four states: California, New York, Texas, and Florida.[47]
- ❏ Of the 18.7 million Latinos immigrants in our country, 5.3 million or 28 percent live in California.[48]
- ❏ Over 2.9 million or 15 percent of Latino immigrants live in Texas.[49]
- ❏ 2.1 million or 11 percent of Latino immigrants live in Florida.[50]
- ❏ 1.3 million or 7 percent of Latino immigrants in the United States live in New York.[51]
- ❏ The highest concentrations of Mexican immigrants are in the West and South. Almost 6 million Mexican immigrants have settled in the West, with over 4 million living in California. The majority of the nearly 4 million Mexican immigrants in the South live in Texas (2.5 million).[52]

Do Latino immigrants speak English well?

- ❏ Latino immigrants' English proficiency varies significantly between adults (eighteen years or older) and their children (five to seventeen years old): 30 percent of adults compared to 68 percent of children speak only English at home or speak it very well.[53]
- ❏ Only one-in-three Latino immigrant children "speak English less than well" compared to seven-in-ten adults.[54]
- ❏ Over half of Caribbean and South American immigrants speak only English at home or speak it very well.[55]

- Only 19 percent of Mexican immigrants and 17 percent of other Central American immigrants don't speak English at all.[56]

What is the age breakdown of Latino immigrants?

The median age of Latino immigrants is thirty-nine years old compared to only eighteen years old for U.S.-born Latinos.[57]

- Only 7 percent of all Latino immigrants are children, while the remaining 93 percent are eighteen and older.[58]
- Less than 7 percent of all Latino children in the nation are immigrants.[59]
- Of all Latino seniors sixty-five years and older, 55 percent are immigrants.[60]

What is the makeup of Latino immigrant families?

- The average size of Latino immigrant families is 4.4 people and varies among Latino origin groups, from 3.8 persons for Caribbean immigrants to 4.7 for Mexican immigrants. Among all Latinos average family size is smaller—3.27 people.[61]
- Over three-fourths (77 percent) of Latino immigrant households include children under the age of eighteen years.[62]
- 4.5 million Latino children under 18 years of age have at least one parent who is an unauthorized immigrant.[63]

How well educated are Latino immigrants?

- Half of all Latino immigrants are high school graduates. The numbers of high school graduates is higher among South Americans (83 percent) and Caribbean immigrants (73 percent).[64]
- One quarter of Latino immigrants attended or graduated from college.[65]

Do most Latino immigrants work?

Over 70 percent of all Latin American immigrants sixteen and older work. The labor participation rate is even higher among male immigrants (83 percent) but lower among female immigrants (58 percent).[66]

- The median annual household income in 2010 for all Latino immigrants was $38,238.[67]

Do all immigrants pay taxes?

- Latino citizens and documented immigrants are subject to the same tax obligations as any American citizen.

Contrary to popular belief, undocumented immigrants also pay taxes. In 2010, unauthorized immigrants contributed $10.6 billion to state and local sales tax, property tax (even if they rent), and income taxes in 2010.[68]

- Many unauthorized immigrants also pay federal income taxes using false Social Security numbers even though they may not file income tax returns.[69]
- Some unauthorized immigrant taxpayers are granted an IRS Individual Taxpayer Identification Number (ITIN) in order to file returns, and this group paid an estimated $9 billion in payroll taxes in 2010. Those taxpayers, 85 percent of whom are Latino, are also eligible for the Additional Child Tax Credit (ACTC) issued to the lowest-income taxpayers with children. In 2010, $4.2 billion was refunded to all ITIN taxpayers claiming the ACTC.[70]

Are undocumented immigrants eligible for government benefits and services?

- Undocumented immigrants are not eligible for

government benefits such as Medicaid, Social Security benefits, and Temporary Assistance to Needy Families.[71]

□ Even authorized immigrants are not eligible for most public benefits for the first five years after entry into the United States. The five-year ban extends to the Supplemental Nutrition Assistance Program (SNAP, formerly the Food Stamp Program), Temporary Assistance for Needy Families (TNAF), Medicaid, Supplemental Security Insurance (SSI), and Children's Health Insurance Program (CHIP).[72]

□ The Emergency Medical Treatment and Labor Act of 1986 and its regulations, however, guarantee that no person shall be deprived of emergency medical treatment on the basis of citizenship, legal status, or ability to pay. As a result, undocumented immigrants may not be turned away from the emergency room.[73]

How are state governments navigating their relationship with undocumented immigrants?

□ Arizona's infamous SB 1070 (Support Our Law Enforcement and Safe Neighborhoods Act), enacted in 2010, which made undocumented immigration a state misdemeanor, barred local and state officials from limiting federal immigration law enforcement and imposed penalties on harboring or hiring undocumented immigrants, was challenged in the courts by the U.S. Department of Justice. In 2012 the U.S. Supreme Court struck down three provisions but upheld the provision allowing law enforcement officers to inquire about immigration status during a lawful stop.[74]

□ In the first half of 2013, lawmakers in forty-three states and the District of Columbia enacted 146 laws and 231 resolutions related to immigration, for a total of 377 pieces of legislation.[75]

□ Legislation in fifteen states extends in-state tuition benefits to unauthorized immigrant students.[76]

- Forty-four states have enacted sixty-nine laws related to immigration and driver's licenses and identification from the beginning of 2011 through June of 2013.[77]
- Other issues addressed by state immigration laws include health, budgetary allocations, human trafficking, employment, and a variety of education issues.[78]

How do Americans view immigrants and immigration reform?

A striking majority of Americans—69 percent of Republicans and 81 percent of Democrats—agree, "Most undocumented immigrants are hard workers who should have the opportunity to stay in this country and improve their lives."[79]

- While a strong majority of Americans believe that unauthorized immigrants should be allowed to remain in the country legally, Americans are divided about offering a pathway to citizenship and prioritizing border security.[80]
- The general public is nearly three times as likely as Latinos (29 percent versus 10 percent) to favor prioritizing better border security and stronger enforcement of immigration laws to deal with unauthorized immigration.[81]
- 45 percent of Latino adults say the impact of unauthorized immigration on Latinos already living in the United States is positive.[82]
- Latinos are almost twice as likely as the general public (42 percent versus 24 percent) to place a priority on creating a path to citizenship for the nation's unauthorized immigrants.[83]
- However, 55 percent of Latinos also agree that relief from the threat of deportation is more important than creating a path to citizenship for unauthorized immigrants.[84]
- Three out of four Americans think that in order to

remain legally in the United States, undocumented immigrants must be proficient in English.[85]

◻ While African Americans share White concerns about the impact of immigration on "traditional American values," they are "far more sympathetic to the plight of immigrants than Whites."[86]

◻ Internationally, polls reveal that Americans are more welcoming to immigrants than Europeans.[87]

◻ The Deferred Action for Childhood Arrivals program provides relief from deportation of unauthorized immigrants younger than thirty who were brought into the country as children and who are currently enrolled in school or have obtained a high school diploma or passed the GED test. Most Latinos (89 percent)—and 86 percent of Latino registered voters—say they approve of this new immigration program.[88]

◻ 31 percent of Latino adults say they know someone who has applied or is planning to apply to the Deferred Action for Childhood Arrivals program. Among Latino registered voters, 26 percent say they know someone who might be eligible for the program and has applied or is planning to do so.[89]

◻ There are approximately 1.4 million "DREAMers" in the United States, that is, young immigrants who might meet the requirements of the deferred action initiative, either now or when they are older.[90]

What are the economic implications of Latino immigration for the future?

◻ Proposed immigration reform that would allow many undocumented immigrants to gain legal status, such as the Senate's 2013 Border Security, Economic Opportunity, and Immigration Modernization Act, if passed by the full Congress would reduce the federal budget deficit by $158 billion in the first ten years and by $685 billion in the second decade according to the Congressional Budget Office.[91]

- The "dependency ratio" measures the numbers of dependent children and elderly for every one hundred workers. The lower the ratio, the lower the per-worker cost for supporting the young and elderly. By 2050, the dependency ratio is estimated to increase to seventy-two out of one hundred from fifty-nine out of one hundred in 2005. With an aging White population, immigration is crucial to keeping the dependency ratio and the costs to workers down.[92]

Voting is a collective and historic action that often compels people to really look at and take a stand on the issues that they and their families, friends, and communities face every day. We do not have to just watch (or ignore) the news and bemoan our plights as if we're powerless to do anything about it.

—Rosario Dawson, actress and co-founder of Voto Latino

With good reason, researchers refer to the growing Latino electorate as an "awakening giant." A significant and courted share of the electorate already, Latinos made up 11 percent of eligible voters in 2012 and are expected to increase their numbers by 40 percent by 2030. Still, as we saw in the 2012 elections, Latinos are not exercising their voting power to its fullest. As a group, Latino nonvoters are young, have just a high school education or less, and earn less money. As they age and the number of Latinos going to college and earning more money continues to rise, voter turnout is likely to increase as well. Though the Voting Rights Act cured historical voter suppression policies and tactics, such as English-only registration and ballot materials, new tactics to undermine full voter participation continue to emerge. Latinos and other committed Americans are challenging and increasingly removing these barriers. A diverse electorate, the Latino population's views on social and political issues varies among the different national origin groups. Progressive on many issues, and conservative on some, Latinos stand to play a crucial role in our polarized political system.

SNAP STATS

A record-breaking 23.7 million Latinos were eligible to vote in the 2012 presidential election. Less than half of them turned out to vote. They voted overwhelmingly for Obama, with just about one in four casting votes for Romney.

More than half of all Latinos are not eligible to vote because they are under age eighteen or non-citizens. That is a much higher share than Whites, Blacks, and Asian Americans. Each year, however, about 800,000 young Latino citizens turn eighteen.

Seven out of ten Latino registered voters identify with or lean towards the Democratic Party. Only one in five favors the Republican Party. The top three issues for Latino voters in the 2012 elections were: education, jobs and the economy, and healthcare. Immigration came in sixth. On social issues, compared to the general public, Latinos are more conservative about abortion, equally accepting of homosexuality, and more supportive of interracial and interethnic marriage.

National origin plays a key role in the diversity of political affiliation and turnout of Latino voters. Voter turnout rates are much higher for Cubans than Mexicans. Cubans, a smaller share of the Latino population than Mexicans or Puerto Ricans, are less likely to lean towards the Democratic Party. The more numerous Mexicans and Puerto Ricans, on the other hand, overwhelmingly affiliate with Democrats.

Latinos are under-represented in federal and state elected positions. Only three Latinos are U.S. senators and twenty-eight hold seats in the House of Representatives. Just two states have Latino governors.

How many Latinos are eligible to vote?

◻ A record 23.7 million Latinos were eligible to vote in the 2012 presidential election, an increase of more than 4 million, or 22 percent, since 2008.[1]

◻ Of all Latinos, 55 percent are not eligible to vote because they are under age eighteen or non-citizens. By comparison, 21 percent of Whites, 31 percent of African Americans, and 46 percent of Asians are ineligible to vote.[2]

◻ In 2012, 17.6 million Latinos were under the age of eighteen and were not eligible to vote.[3]

◻ Among the 3.8 million young Latinos who became eligible to vote between 2008 and 2012, 3.7 million were born in the United States.[4]

◻ Around 800,000 Latinos turn eighteen each year and this number is estimated to grow to one million per year adding an estimated 16 million new Latino voters by 2030.[5]

◻ The 5.4 million Latino immigrants who have green cards now will also add to the voter rolls as they become naturalized citizens in the future. Immigration reform may also have an impact on the number of Latinos who become eligible for citizenship and eventually gain voting rights.[6]

◻ By 2030, with a growth rate of 40 percent, the Latino electorate is expected to reach 40 million, almost doubling it.[7]

How many Latinos are registered to vote?

◻ Latinos accounted for 10.8 percent of all registered voters in 2012.[8] According to a study of the Latino electorate conducted by the Pew Research Center, the number of Latinos who said they were registered to vote in 2012 reached 13.7 million, up 18 percent over 2008.[9]

□ An additional 8.6 million Latinos were eligible to register to vote (eighteen years old or older and American citizens), but were not registered.[10]

How many Latino citizens turned out to vote in the 2012 presidential election?

A record 11.2 million Latinos voted in the 2012 presidential election, 48 percent of Latino eligible voters, down from 49.9 percent in 2008. Twelve million eligible voters did not come out to vote.[11]

□ Latinos make up 8.4 percent of all Americans who voted in 2012, up from 7.4 percent in 2008.[12]

□ In 2012, the Latino voter turnout rate declined for nearly all major Latino demographic groups with the exception of three:

- The voter turnout rate of naturalized Latino immigrants who arrived in the 1990s increased from 41.2 percent in 2008 to 47.2 percent in 2012.
- Among Latinos ages sixty-five and older, the voter turnout rate increased from 56 percent in 2008 to 59.9 percent in 2012.
- The voter turnout rate of Puerto Ricans increased from 49.7 percent in 2008 to 52.8 percent in 2012.[13]

□ In 2012, 70.8 percent of Latinos with a college degree and 67.2 percent of Latinos of Cuban origin voted—both substantially higher than the 48 percent turnout rate among all Latinos. [14]

□ Some of the lowest voter turnout rates among Latino demographic subgroups were among those with less than a high school education (35.3 percent) or just a high school diploma (39.4 percent), young Latinos aged eighteen to twenty-nine (36.9 percent), and Mexicans (42.2).[15]

□ Latino women voted at a higher rate than men— 49.8 percent versus 46 percent.[16]

- Latinos who are naturalized citizens voted at a higher rate than those born in the United States—53.6 percent versus 46.1 percent.[17]
- Among Latino immigrants, 58.8 percent of those who arrived before 1990 voted, while voter turnout rates were lower among those who arrived between 1990 and 1999 as well as those who arrived after 2000— 47.2 percent and 44.1 percent respectively.[18]

For whom did Latinos vote in the 2012 presidential election?

- President Barack Obama garnered 71 percent of the Latino vote, while Mitt Romney received only 27 percent.[19]

Latinos made up a growing number of voters in three battleground states in that election: Florida (14 percent), Nevada (18 percent), and Colorado (14 percent).[20]

- Obama received 76 percent of the female Latino vote and 65 percent of the male Latino vote.[21]
- Of young Latino voters, 74 percent supported Obama compared to 60 percent of all young voters.[22]
- 82 percent of Latino voters with household income of $50,000 or less voted for Obama.[23]
- Obama enjoyed a smaller majority among Latinos with college degrees: 59 percent.[24]

What are Latinos' political party affiliations?

- Seven out of ten Latino registered voters identify with or lean towards the Democratic Party (70 percent), while only 22 percent favor the Republican Party.[25]
- Overall, religious affiliation does not have the same impact on party affiliation among Latinos as it does among White voters.
  - 71 percent of Latino Catholics (who make up

57 percent of the Latino electorate) favor the Democratic Party, compared to 47 percent of White Catholics.[26]

- More than half of Latino Evangelicals (52 percent) favor the Democratic Party, compared to only 23 percent of White Evangelicals.[27]
- Almost three-quarters of White Evangelicals (72 percent) identify or lean towards the Republican Party, while only 36 percent of Latino Evangelicals do.[28]

▫ Among religiously unaffiliated Latino voters, eight in ten are Democrats or lean towards the Democratic Party.[29]

▫ In 2013, two Latinos were high level officials of the Democratic Party:

- Maria Elena Durazo, Vice Chair of the Democratic Party
- Henry R. Muñoz III, National Finance Committee Chair[30]

▫ Eight hundred Latinos were delegates to the 2012 Democratic Party convention.[31]

What are the obstacles to Latino voter participation?

▫ Many historical obstacles to Latinos registering and voting, such as poll taxes, "shady registration practices," and English-only ballot materials, were removed by the Voting Rights Act of 1964, as amended in 1975 to include "language minorities."[32]

▫ In advance of the 2012 elections, at least 130 state bills were introduced that would make voter registration and voting more difficult, limit voter registration drives, and disenfranchise citizens with prior criminal convictions. With a disproportionate impact on African Americans and Latinos as well as young and low-income people, nineteen of the bills became law and sixty-nine were defeated.[33]

▫ In 2013, eight states passed nine bills restricting voter access, but ten states passed thirteen laws expanding access.[34]

- Laws requiring voters to present photo identification at the polls are one key restrictive tactic since these laws were recently introduced into states with high minority turnout and larger African American and non-citizen populations.[35] Today, eleven states have laws requiring photo identification that at least one in ten voters don't have: Florida, Georgia, Hawaii, Idaho, Indiana, Kansas, Louisiana, Michigan, New Hampshire, South Dakota, and Tennessee. Together, these states are home to 15 percent of all Latino eligible voters.[36]

- State felony disenfranchisement laws prevent almost 6 million American citizens with prior convictions from voting. Data on African Americans reveals that one in every thirteen is deprived of their right to vote as a result. While similar data is not available for Latinos, data on their disproportionate numbers of convictions suggest a similarly disparate impact.[37]

Are Latinos' political views more progressive or conservative than other Americans' views?

- Latinos are more likely to identify as progressive (30 percent) than the general American public (21 percent).[38]

- Latinos characterize their political views as conservative (32 percent) at about the same rate as the general public (34 percent).[39]

When it comes to government's size and role, many more Latinos (75 percent) favor "bigger government providing more services" over "smaller government with fewer services" than the general American public (41 percent).[40]

What are Latinos' views on key social and economic issues in the political arena?

- The top three issues for Latino voters in the 2012

elections were: education (50 percent), jobs and the economy (49 percent), and health care (45 percent). Immigration came in sixth place (34 percent).[41]

▫ Latino adults, including nonvoters, ranked the same top three issues as most important to them. Immigration ranked fourth.[42]

▫ On social issues, compared to the general public, Latinos are more conservative about abortion, equally accepting of homosexuality, and more supportive of interracial and interethnic marriage.[43]

  ▪ Of the Latino population, 51 percent are opposed to abortion in most cases, compared to 41 percent of the general public.[44]

  ▪ Of the Latino population, 58 percent agree that homosexuality should be accepted by society compared to 59 percent of the general public.[45]

  ▪ Latinos are more likely to support interracial and interethnic marriages (48 percent) than Whites (40 percent), but a little less than African Americans (51 percent).[46]

▫ While just half of all American voters believe that climate change is already happening, three quarters of Latino voters do. 86 percent of Latinos favor President Obama taking action to reduce pollution that causes climate change.[47]

How many Latinos are in the U.S. Senate and House of Representatives?

▫ While Latinos were estimated to be 17 percent of the population in 2012, they are only 3 percent of the one hundred senators and 6 percent of the 435 representatives in the House of Representatives.[48]

▫ Thirty-one Latinos were elected to the U.S. Congress in the 2012 elections.[49] A record-breaking three Latinos were elected to the U.S. Senate in 2012: Republican Ted Cruz was elected to his first term from Texas, Republican Marco Rubio from Florida, and Democrat Robert Menendez from New Jersey were re-elected.[50]

- Twenty-eight Latinos now sit in the U.S. House of Representatives.[51]

How many political appointees in the Obama administration are Latino?

- Secretary of Labor Thomas E. Perez is the only Latino member of Obama's second-term cabinet.[52]
- In Obama's first term, he appointed two Latinos to his cabinet: Hilda Solis, Secretary of Labor, and Ken E. Salazar, Secretary of the Interior.[53]
- Only 7 percent of the 4,000 political appointees named by President Obama and listed in the 2012 "Plum Book," are Latino according to National Latino Leadership Agenda estimates.[54]
- Five of the top 53 political appointees (not including cabinet members) profiled on the official White House blog pages are Latino: Felicia Escobar (Senior Policy Director for Immigration), Cecilia Muñoz (Assistant to the President and Director of the Domestic Policy Council), Julie Chavez Rodriguez (Deputy Director of Public Engagement), Daniel Suvor (Senior Director of the Office of Cabinet Affairs), and Katherine Vargas (Director of Latino Media).[55]

How many Latinos are judges at the federal and state levels?

In 2009, President Barack Obama appointed Associate Justice Sonya Sotomayor to the Supreme Court of the United States. She is the first Latina to be appointed to the bench.[56]

- Currently, 116 Latino judges serve in the federal courts, or about 13 percent of the 874 federal judgeships.[57]
- In his first five years in office, President Obama nominated twenty-seven Latinos to the federal courts,

George W. Bush appointed thirty Latinos to the federal bench over his full two terms, and William Clinton appointed twenty-three.[58]

□ As of 2009, at the state level fewer than four hundred Latino judges served in a total of twenty-three states.[59]

How many Latinos hold elected positions in the United States?

□ In 2011, 5,850 Latinos were serving in elected offices.[60]

The four states with the largest number of Latino elected officials were Texas, California, New Mexico, and Arizona. However, there was rapid growth in regions outside the Southwest, including Illinois, New Jersey, and other states with emerging Latino populations.[61]

□ Nine Latinos serve in statewide offices, including the office of governor.[62]

□ As of 2013, only two Latinos served as governor: Susana Martinez of New Mexico and Brian Sandoval of Nevada. Governor Martinez is the first Latina governor in U.S. history.[63]

□ As of 2012, there were 352 Latino state legislators, 219 Democrats, and 44 Republicans.[64]

□ Regionally, the Northeast had the most Latino state legislators with 142. Among the fifty states, New Mexico had the most Latino legislators with forty, followed by California with twenty-three.[65]

How many cities have Latino mayors?

□ Across the United States, there were 240 Latino mayors in fifteen states in 2013.[66]

□ Five major cities had Latino mayors in 2013: Newark, NJ; Miami, FL; Providence, RI; San Antonio, TX; and Hartford, CT.[67]

What are Latino views on national Latino leadership?

- When asked in an open-ended question to name the nation's most important Latino leader, most Latinos say either that they don't know (62 percent) or "no one" (9 percent).[68]
- Three-quarters of Latinos see the need for national Latino leaders to advance the concerns of the U.S. Latino community.[69]
- Among those Latinos who did name someone when asked who is "the most important Latino leader in the country today," 5 percent named Justice Sonia Sotomayor and an equal number answered Senator Marco Rubio, 3 percent named former Los Angeles mayor Antonio Villaraigosa, and 2 percent said U.S. Representative from Chicago, Luis Gutierrez.[70]

If it were a standalone country, the U.S. Hispanic market buying power would make it one of the top twenty economies in the world.

—*Nielsen*, State of the Hispanic Consumer

Depictions of Latinos as "poor and needy" are based on some truths but miss the mark. A look at the numbers debunks many dated misconceptions. Yes, too many Latinos face high poverty rates, endure employment discrimination, and are often relegated to low wage jobs. The Great Recession demolished more than half of Latino wealth and foreclosures took a substantial portion of their homes. While still very much in recovery, this sizeable and youthful population is actually expanding economic growth in the United States. More than half of new homeowners in 2012 were Latino, helping to fuel the recovery. Latinos contribute billions of dollars in taxes and to the GDP. Though they earn less, Latinos are less likely than White Americans to take advantage of government benefit programs and receive less assistance when they do. The 15 million Latinos earning over $50,000 annually are young and key contributors to Latinos' trillion dollar buying power. These days they are the apple of the advertising industry's eye. With rising rates of educational attainment, more Latinos have a chance at upward mobility. But is this enough to overcome the steep economic inequalities of this country?

SNAP STATS

Nearly 25 million Latinos account for 16 percent of the U.S. workforce. With the youngest median age out of any racial/ethnic group, the Latino workforce is growing—rapidly. Between 2012 and 2013 alone, the Latino workforce grew by 3 million and is set to be at 19 percent of the total U.S. workforce by the year 2020.

Latinos earn less than other Americans. With a median annual household income at $39,000, Latinos earn $11,000 less than the median for the total U.S. population and have the lowest weekly earnings out of any other group.

The Great Recession hit the Latino community hard. Losing jobs and homes, Latino wealth (assets minus liability) decreased by nearly 44 percent during the Great Recession. Though jobs have been added to the economy and the unemployment rate is down, in states like California, where Latinos will soon be the racial/ethnic majority, unemployment remains at recession rates.

Latinos receive less of the nation's entitlement benefits (Social Security, Medicare, etc.) than White Americans. While 17 percent of the population, Latinos receive only 12 percent of all government benefits, compared to 69 percent for White Americans who represent 75 percent of the population. Latinos do receive SNAP benefits ("food stamps") at a slightly higher rate than Whites, and accept Medicaid in line with their share of the U.S. population despite their higher poverty levels.

Latinos are homeowners. Nearly half of Latinos own their own home, but that is still a lower share than the two-thirds of all Americans who own their homes. This is changing as Latinos accounted for more than half of the increase of homeowners in 2012.

With rising numbers, Latinos are becoming the face of small business. In 2013 alone, 3.1 million Latino small businesses contributed a projected $468 billion to the American economy. Their numbers are growing with Latina entrepreneurs starting small businesses at a much higher rate than the national average.

Latino buying power is at one trillion dollars annually and will grow by more than 50 percent by 2015. With salsa replacing ketchup as America's number one condiment and tortilla sales topping hot dog and hamburger bun sales, advertisers invested nearly $8 billion in the Latino market in 2012.

BY THE NUMBERS . . .

EMPLOYMENT AND MILITARY SERVICE

How many Latinos are in the U.S. workforce?

- There are nearly 25 million Latinos, sixteen and over, in the United States civilian labor force.[1]
- Of the entire U.S. Labor force, 16 percent is Latino.[2]
- From 2012 to 2013 the Latino labor force grew by 3 million.[3]
- The Department of Labor predicts that by 2020 Latinos will account for 19 percent of the labor force.[4]
- 67.4 percent of Latinos sixteen and older were in the civilian labor force in 2011.[5]
- Making up 42 percent of the unskilled American labor force, Latino immigrants come to the United States to do many of the jobs that native unskilled workers of all races and ethnicities do not want to do, such as janitors and housekeepers and farm workers. Native-born unskilled workers prefer jobs such as funeral workers and crossing guards.[6]

What are Latino rates of employment and unemployment?

- There were 22,741,000 employed Latinos at the end of 2013.[7]

- In 2012, four out of five employed Latinos were employed full time.[8]
- The unemployment rate for Latinos was at 9 percent compared to 6.3 percent for Whites and 12.9 percent for African Americans.[9]
- As of September 2013, around 2.2 million Latino workers were unemployed, 19 percent of all unemployed workers.[10]
- The average duration of unemployment for Latinos was less than the average for the total population at nearly thirty-seven weeks, almost three weeks shorter than the duration for African Americans.[11]
- Though Latino workers experienced less long-term unemployment than the general population, the rate of long-term unemployment increased dramatically from .8 percent in 2007 to 4.9 percent in 2010.[12]
- Much like the larger U.S. population, Latino youth ages 16 to 19 suffer from the highest rates of unemployment at about 31 percent.[13]
- By the end of 2012, northeastern states had the highest rates of Latino unemployment with Rhode Island leading the country at 18 percent.[14]
- In 2012, of the states with the highest population of Latinos, Texas, with over 10 million Latino residents, had the lowest Latino unemployment rate at 7.7 percent, while California, with over 14 million Latino residents, saw the highest rate at 12.7 percent.[15]
- A little over 18 percent of Latinos are underemployed.[16]
- Latinas have an employment to population ratio of 52.7 percent, significantly lower than Latino males (79.2 percent), and the lowest of any demographic group.[17]
- Latinos lost 473,000 jobs in the recession but gained 1.3 million jobs in the recovery.[18]

What types of jobs do Latinos hold?

Nearly one in four Latinos work in the construction industry.[19]

- Latino workers are also an integral part of other industry workforces as well, such as:
  - 22.5 percent of agriculture
  - 21.9 percent of leisure and hospitality
  - 17.5 percent of the mining industry
  - 16.8 percent of wholesale trade
  - 16.2 percent of transportation and utilities[20]
- With the exception of construction, of the fastest growing industries, Latinos only make up 7.1 percent of professional, scientific, and technical services jobs, 9.5 percent of education services jobs, and 10.9 percent of health and social assistance jobs, the fastest growing industry (projected to grow by 5.6 million jobs by 2020). [21]
- Over 2.5 million Latinas work in sales and office occupations.[22]
- According to the U.S. Department of Agriculture, there were just over one million farmworkers in this country in 2012. Of these workers, 68 percent were Mexican, and 3 percent were Central American, a majority of whom are immigrants.[23]
- Latina women, particularly immigrants, are disproportionately represented (41 percent) in maid and housekeeping occupations, among the top six high-risk injury professions in the United States.[24]
- In 2011, 19.2 percent of employed Latinos sixteen and older worked in management, business, science, and arts occupations.[25]
- There are 77,440 Latino CEOs.[26]
- In 2013, there were 50,866 Latino physicians and surgeons.[27]

How many Latinos work in the private sector?

- Latinos are more likely to work in the private sector

than African Americans and Whites; eight in ten Latinos work in the private sector.[28]

What percentage of Latinos work in the public and nonprofit sector?

- Latinos are only 10 percent of the employees of state, local, or federal agencies, a smaller share than African Americans (19 percent), and Whites (14 percent).[29]
- Latinos account for only 8.2 percent of the permanent federal workforce; African Americans make up 18 percent, with Whites accounting for the majority of the permanent federal civilians employees at around 65.4 percent.[30]
- The federal agencies with the largest percentage of Latinos in their workforce are:
  - Department of Homeland Security at 20.9 percent
  - Social Security Administration at 14.5 percent
  - Equal Employment Opportunity Commission at 13.6 percent
  - Department of the Treasury at 9.5 percent[31]
- Latinos are severely underrepresented in mid to upper management positions in foundations:
  - 3 percent of foundation CEOs and presidents
  - 4 percent of full-time executive staff
  - 11 percent of program officers, the only management position in which their share reaches double digits
  - 5 percent of board members and trustees.[32]

How many Latinos serve in the military?

- There are 157,206 Latinos in active duty in the military, roughly 11.3 percent of all active duty personnel.[33]
- Latinos are 12.5 percent of the U.S. Air Force.[34]
- Of active duty and reserve sailors in the navy, 58,000 or 13 percent are Latino.[35]

- Latinos are 13.6 percent of the U.S. Marine Corps, up from 9 percent in 1995.[36]
- Across the different military branches, only 5 percent of all officers are Latino, lagging behind African Americans (8 percent, also underrepresented) and Whites (77 percent).[37]
- There are 1.2 million Latino veterans of the U.S. armed forces.[38] One in five veterans of both Gulf Wars is Latino.[39]
- 3 percent of Latino veterans are not U.S. citizens.[40]
- Latino veterans have an unemployment rate of 8.2 percent, lower than African American vets (10 percent), but higher than White vets (6.4 percent).[41]
- Though the Latino unemployment rate for veterans hovers below the national average, Latino veterans from the second Iraq War have unemployment rates in the double digits at nearly 12 percent.[42]
- 9.7 percent of Latino veterans are living in poverty.[43]
- There are twenty-seven Latino Medal of Honor recipients; interestingly, 33 percent of those medals are from the Korean War alone.[44]

EARNINGS AND POVERTY

How much money do Latinos earn?

The median household income for Latinos in the United States is $39,000, $11,000 less than the median income for the total U.S. population.[45]

- With a median household income of $35,900, Latino immigrants earn less than U.S. born Latinos who earn a median income of $42,500.[46]
- Latinas with bachelor's degrees earn $31,720 less than White males with bachelor's degrees.[47]
- Increasing the federal minimum wage to $10.10 by 2015 would benefit nearly 25 percent of Latinos.[48]

In 2012, Latinos working full time earned an average of $568 a week, $200 less a than the average for all full-time American workers.[49]

□ At an average of $521 a week, Latino women have the lowest weekly earnings of any demographic group, male or female. Latino men have the second lowest weekly wages at an average $592 per week out of any group, male or female.[50]

□ Between 2007 and 2012, among full-time worker weekly earnings:

- Full-time Latino male workers' weekly wages increased by 2.8 percent, compared to 0.7 percent increase for all full-time male workers.
- Between 2007 and 2012, while Latino men's weekly wages increased at a higher rate than all American male workers, Latinas' weekly wages decreased by .5 percent compared to all American female workers who saw 1.6 percent increase.[51]

Latino households that earn $50,000 or more are growing at a faster rate than all American households. Between 2000 and 2011:

- The number of Latino households with earnings between $50,000 and $74,900 grew by 10 percent, while households with earnings at that level for the total U.S. population saw very little growth.
- Latino households with earnings of $75,000 through $100,000 grew by 31 percent compared to the 16 percent growth seen in the number of all American households at the same level.
- Latino households earning more than $100,000 saw a 70 percent increase, while the total number of households earning at the same level increased by 49 percent.[52]

How many Latinos live in poverty?

- The poverty rate for Latinos in 2011 was 25.6 percent, down from 26.5 percent in 2010.[53]
- Slightly more Mexicans (27 percent) live in poverty than other Latinos.[54]
- 70.1 percent of Latinos aged sixty-five and older have incomes less than two times the supplemental poverty threshold, the threshold for the most basic level of subsistence.[55]
- 24 percent of all Latino immigrants live in poverty compared to 28 percent of Mexican immigrants.[56]
- Nearly 39 percent of Latino immigrant children under the age of eighteen live in poverty.[57]

WORKPLACE SAFETY AND DISCRIMINATION

Are Latinos more at risk for injury and death at the workplace than other Americans?

- At 4.4 per 100,000 workers, Latinos have the highest work-related fatal injury rates.[58]
- The rate of work-related fatalities has declined for all Latinos. From 2009 to 2010, native-born Latinos share of work-related fatalities went down by a little over 10 percent, a significantly higher decrease than that of Latino immigrants who saw a mere 1 percent drop.[59]
- Latinas represented 10.2 percent of the total workplace fatalities for women in 2010. Half of all the Latinas who died in the workplace were victims of assaults and violent acts.[60]
- Nearly a quarter of Latinos work in high-risk occupations, with considerable overrepresentation (41 percent) in maid and housekeeping occupations, among the top six high-risk injury professions.[61]
- Between 1998 and 2007, 27 percent of all adolescents (aged fifteen through seventeen) who died on the job were Latino.[62]

□ In 2012, almost 12 percent of workers suffering non-fatal work related injuries and illnesses requiring time off were Latino, 40 percent were White, and 8 percent were African American. Though Latino workers had a lower reported incidence rate than Whites, their required time off from work averaged nine days compared to Whites who lost seven days.[63]

Do Latinos experience discrimination in the workplace?

□ 22 percent of Latinos reported feeling discriminated against in their current job, compared to 25 percent of African Americans and 22 percent of disabled workers.[64]

Around 33 percent of all Latinos in three major cities (New York, Los Angeles, and Chicago) work for less than the minimum wage, compared to 8 percent of their White colleagues. Latino immigrants (35 percent) and women (40 percent) suffer even greater rates of minimum wage theft.[65]

□ Latino workers experience overtime pay violations more than any other ethnic group. 77.6 percent of Latinos surveyed in minimum wage industries did not receive earned overtime pay.[66]

□ Latinas often work in professions with higher rates of sexual harassment. One-third of all sexual harassment cases in 2011 were in the restaurant industry where 22 percent of the workers are Latino.[67]

□ In domestic work, Latinas not only face higher rates of sexual harassment but are also often threatened and physically abused.[68]

□ One survey revealed that 72 percent of Latina farmworkers in the South reported that sexual harassment was a problem for them at work.[69]

□ 30 percent of Latino transgendered and gender non-conforming workers report losing jobs "due to their gender identity/expression." Another 47 percent believe that they were not hired for jobs due to the same bias.[70]

UNIONS AND BUSINESS OWNERS

How many Latino workers are in labor unions?

- Of all union members, 9.8 percent are Latino.[71]
- While African Americans have a higher share of union membership, Latino union members average higher weekly earnings than they do.[72]
- Latino union members earn 51 percent more than their non-union counterparts, compared to African Americans who earn only 31 percent, and Whites who earn 23 percent more than their non-union counterparts.[73]

How many Latinos are self-employed or small business owners?

A total of 3.1 million Latino-owned businesses contributed more than $468 billion to the American economy in 2013.[74]

- In 2013, 17 percent of California's small business owners were Latino and added $100 billion to the economy annually, while contributing 650,000 jobs.[75]
- 9.1 percent of Latinos are self-employed compared to 7.8 percent of the general U.S. population.[76]

The amount of Latino-owned businesses grew by close to 7 percent from 2007 to 2013.[77]

- Latina entrepreneurs are starting small businesses at a rate that is six times the national average.[78]
- 56 percent of Latino business owners have household incomes of more than $50,000. Latino business

owners are also 66 percent more likely than Latinos generally to earn between $100,000 and $149,000.[79]

REMITTANCES, GOVERNMENT ASSISTANCE, AND TAXES

Do Latinos send remittances to countries outside the United States?

◻ Of foreign remittances received in Mexico, 98 percent or nearly $22 billion come from U.S. residents, accounting for almost 2 percent of Mexico's GDP.[80]

The United States is the largest source of remittances sent to seventeen Spanish-speaking Latin American countries (including Mexico), sending $41 billion of the $52.9 billion (78 percent) received in the region.[81]

How many Latinos participate in government assistance programs?

In 2011 Whites received 69 percent of the nation's total entitlement benefits (e.g., Social Security and SNAP, also known as "food stamps"), while Latinos received only 12 percent.[82]

◻ Of all Latinos, 22 percent participated in SNAP, compared to 9 percent of Whites, 7 percent of Asians, and 28 percent of African Americans.[83]
◻ In 2011, among Latinos receiving Social Security retirement benefits, 44 percent of elderly married couples and 61 percent of elderly unmarried persons relied on Social Security for 90 percent or more of their income.[84]
◻ Similar to the gender gap in the larger U.S. population, 31 percent of Latinas compared to 14 per-

cent of Latino men stated that they have received assistance.[85]

- 17 percent of Latinas receive Medicaid compared to 9 percent of White women.[86]

How much do Latinos pay in taxes?

- As 16 percent of the U.S. labor force, Latinos contribute proportionately to the nation's tax revenues.[87] As noted earlier:
  - Contrary to what many are led to believe, undocumented immigrant workers do pay taxes. In 2010, they contributed $10.6 billion to state and local sales, property (even if they rent), and income taxes in 2010.[88]
  - Many unauthorized immigrants also pay federal income taxes even though they do not have a valid Social Security number.[89]

WEALTH

How are Latinos affected by the U.S. wealth gap?

- The wealth gap between Latinos and White Americans is wider than the income gap.[90]

> **The median wealth of Whites is almost twelve times greater than the wealth of Latinos and fourteen times greater than African Americans.[91]**

- During the Great Recession, Latino wealth (their net worth: assets minus liabilities) went down by 44 percent, significantly more than African Americans and Whites.[92]
- By the end of the Great Recession in 2009, the wealth of Whites was eighteen times greater than that of Latinos.[93]

□ The average net worth of Latino households slipped from $18,359 in 2005 to $6,325 in 2009.[94]

□ The wealthiest top 10 percent of Latinos increased their share of the overall wealth of Latinos from 56 percent in 2005 to 72 percent in 2009.[95]

How many Latinos own their home?

□ A little less than half, 46 percent, of Latinos own their homes, a considerably lower share than for all Americans (65 percent).[96]

□ Latinos accounted for 51 percent of the total net increase of homeowners in 2012.[97]

Of Mexicans, 49 percent are homeowners, the highest homeownership rate for all Latino groups. Among Mexicans, however, the homeownership of immigrants is below the average of all Latinos at 45 percent, while U.S.-born Mexicans are well above the average at 53 percent.[98]

□ Latinos were hit hard by the foreclosure crisis of the Great Recession. By 2011, the foreclosure rate for Latinos was higher than any other group at 11.9 percent, nearly double the rate of White Americans.[99]

□ 56 percent of Latinos view homeownership as a symbol of success and achievement, compared to 32 percent of the general U.S. population.[100]

How many Latino households have a car?

□ In 2011, only 13.5 percent of Latino households did not have access to a car or truck, compared to 9.3 percent of the total U.S. population. The proportion of African American households without a vehicle is double that of the total population.[101]

□ In 2012, Latinos spent $16.2 billion on new vehicle purchases.[102]

- New vehicle sales are rebounding at a faster rate for Latinos than for Americans generally, 26 percent compared to 15 percent respectively.[103]

How many Latinos have savings accounts and retirement plans or accounts?

- 52 percent of Latino households have a savings account compared to 75 percent of White and 52.8 percent of African American households.[104]
- 86 percent of Latinos earning between $50,000 and $100,000 annually maintain a savings account.[105]
- 69 percent of Latinos and 62 percent of African American working-age heads of households do not have any type of retirement savings, while nearly 70 percent of White working-aged households do have retirement accounts.[106]

Only 38 percent of Latino employees aged twenty-five to sixty-four work for an employer who offers a retirement plan, one of the most common investments for workers.[107]

- Four out of five Latino households, aged twenty-five to sixty-four, have retirement savings of less than $10,000, compared to 75 percent of African American and 50 percent of White households.[108]
- In 2010, 11 percent of Latinos, 10 percent of African Americans, and 35 percent of Whites held IRAs and Keogh plans.[109]
- The average retirement account balance of Latino heads of households, aged twenty-five to sixty-four, is $17,600, a mere 16 percent of the average retirement account balance of Whites ($111,749).[110]

Where do Latinos bank and manage their money?

- 48.7 percent of Latino households rely solely on FDIC

insured banks, compared to 41 percent of African Americans and 77 percent of Whites.[111]

□ 20 percent of the population of Latinos and 21 percent of African Americans do not have accounts in FDIC insured banks, but instead use alternatives such as check-cashing businesses, pawnshops, and payday lending firms. This is a substantially higher proportion than Whites (4 percent) and Asians (2.7 percent). [112]

Are Latinos investing?

□ Three in four Latinos believe that owning a home is the best long-term investment possible.[113]

□ The majority of Latinas spend their extra money building financial stability either through paying off debts (73 percent) or increasing their savings (63 percent).[114]

In 2010, 4 percent of Latinos invested in stocks and mutual funds, higher than the 2 percent of African Americans investing in these assets, but significantly lower than the 22 percent of Whites who are in the market.[115]

□ 50 percent of Latinos with annual earnings of $50,000 to $100,000 have investments in stocks and mutual funds.[116]

How much debt do Latinos carry?

□ On average, Latinos have $6,066 worth of credit card debt, a drop of 33 percent since 2008.[117] Though Whites carry more debt ($7,315), they have a lower APR rate (15.8 percent) associated with their debt than Latinos (17.9 percent).[118]

□ 40 percent of Latinos rely on credit cards to make ends meet (i.e., covering basic living expenses such as rent, groceries, mortgage payments, etc.).[119]

> Fewer Latino millennials (69 percent) are in debt than non-Latinos (75 percent) and owe less money: on average Latino millenials are $18,000 in debt while non-Latinos are $27,800 in debt.[120]

- Less than 10 percent of Latinos in debt declare bankruptcy, compared to a general bankruptcy rate of 15 percent. Whites and African Americans declare above the average rate.[121]

How many Latinos serve on corporate boards?

- Latinos hold a slim 3 percent of seats in Fortune 500 company boardrooms.[122]
- Of Fortune 500 companies, 70 percent do not have a Latino on their board.[123]
- Latinas hold less than 1 percent of board seats of Fortune 500 companies.[124]
- Only 4 percent of Fortune 500 companies have two Latinos on their board.[125]
- In 2013, there were only ten Latino CEOs in the Fortune 500.[126]

How much do Latinos give to charity?

- Latino charitable giving is rising: 63 percent of Latino households make charitable donations.[127]
- According to the Bureau of Labor Statistics, around 15 percent of Latinos volunteer their time through or for an organization.[128]
- Consistent with their values, 33 percent of Latinos donate to religious groups.[129]
- Another 19 percent of Latinos contribute to healthcare and social service groups.[130]

THE LATINO CONSUMER

How much buying power do Latinos have?

- Latino buying power is expected to increase from

$1 trillion in 2010[131] to $1.5 trillion in 2015—a 50 percent jump over five years.[132]

◻ According to a study on Latino purchasing decision-making, 86 percent of Latina women indicated that they are the primary shopper in their household.[133]

◻ Salsa has replaced ketchup as America's number one condiment while tortillas continue to outsell both hot dog and hamburger buns.[134]

◻ Latinos spend significantly more than the general market on baby products, hair care, and toiletries. In many cases they are willing to spend as much as 15 percent more than the general market for name brand versions of these products.[135]

◻ From June 2012 till May 2013, Latinas spent around $3.3 billion on fashion footwear, accounting for 18 percent of the total women's fashion footwear market.[136]

◻ 26 percent of Latinas shop via their mobile phones.[137]

How do advertisers market to Latinos?

◻ In 2012, media spending on Latinos in the United States totaled $7.9 billion. With the majority spent on Spanish-language television, advertisement spending increased by 13.5 percent in the first quarter of 2013. Latino magazines realized an increase of 12 percent, while spending in mainstream consumer magazines increased by less than 2 percent.[138]

◻ The top seven advertisers in the Spanish-language market are: Procter & Gamble, McDonald's, AT&T, Verizon, Toyota, General Mills, and General Motors.[139]

◻ There is a strong correlation between language and advertisers' ability to connect with the Latino audience. Nielsen polls reveal four key insights about language and the Latino market:

  ▪ Latinos remember English-language commercials as well as the general population.

- The same commercial shown in Spanish bumps up ad recall by as much as 30 percent.
- Latinos like ads 51 percent more if viewed in Spanish rather than English.
- Hiring Spanish-speaking talent to deliver the script resonates 30 percent better with Latinos.[140]

> Familismo is the value of family over individual or community needs and the expression of strong loyalty, reciprocity, and solidarity among family members.
>
> *—U.S. Centers for Disease Control and Prevention commenting on Latino belief systems in "Cultural Insights: Communicating with Hispanics/Latinos"*

Large, bilingual, multigenerational, and increasingly racially and ethnically diverse, Latino families are central to the happiness and resilience of Latino communities across the country. Most Latinos live in segregated urban neighborhoods with high levels of poverty, pollution, gangs, and crime. Yet the realities they face where they live don't deter Latinos from pursing the activities they love best. Gathering for a meal, going to the movies together, playing and watching sports, and enjoying the outdoors, Latinos actively engage in sustaining relationships with their friends and families. Predominantly Catholic, many also go to church together on Sundays. Even so, growing numbers of Latinos are joining evangelical congregations, and interfaith Latino families are becoming the new normal. Latino families are changing in other ways, too. More Latinos with little formal education are becoming the parents of college graduates. Non-citizen immigrants are the parents and grandparents of rising numbers of children born in the United States. Embracing their changing families, Latinos are not only happy with their lives but optimistic about their ability to shape the future and what it holds for them.

SNAP STATS

Latino family households are larger than the average American family. Latino families are also more likely to span three or more generations, to be bilingual, and more racially and ethnically diverse than other American families.

Less than half of Latinos are married, not surprising given their relative youth as a group. A majority of Latino married couples have children under the age of eighteen, often relying on grandparents for childcare.

Though slightly more than half of Latinos are Catholic, growing numbers are joining evangelical Protestant congregations. One-in-five Latino adults who were raised Catholic leave the church, and almost half of the Latino evangelical population joined the religion as adults.

The average Latino lives in a segregated, lower income neighborhood. Despite the inequalities they deal with in their communities, Latinos are optimistic about the future. Many believe that, ". . . people like me and my family have a good chance of improving our standard of living."

BY THE NUMBERS . . .

FAMILY

How many Latino family households are there in the United States?

- There are 11.6 million Latino family households in the United States.[1]
- Over three-quarters of Latino households are family

households, compared to slightly less than two-thirds of White and African American households.[2]

What is the makeup of Latino families?

◻ The average Latino family has 3.27 members, compared to 2.43 for non-Latinos, a difference of nearly a whole person.[3]

◻ The average Latino immigrant family has 4.4 members per household.[4]

8 percent of Latino families are multigenerational (i.e., consisting of three or more generations), compared to the same percentage for African Americans, but only 3 percent of Whites and 6 percent of Asians.[5]

◻ Latino families are often "mixed-status" families, "that is, a family with at least one undocumented immigrant parent and at least one U.S. citizen child." In 2010 almost half of undocumented immigrants (46 percent) had minor children.[6]

◻ Latinos account for 15.4 percent of same-sex couple households.[7]

◻ There are over 5 million two-parent Latino families (married and unmarried) with children under the age of eighteen.[8]

◻ In 2011, 85.2 percent of Latino children seventeen and younger lived with at least one parent.[9]

◻ The rate of Latino children living in two-parent households dropped from 75 percent in 1980 to 59 percent in 2012.[10]

◻ There are 2.7 million Latino single-parent families with children under the age of eighteen. Of these families, 87 percent are headed by mothers.

◻ 24 percent of Latino children under eighteen years old live with just their mothers compared to

4 percent who lived with just their fathers. A similar gender gap is seen across all ethnic and racial groups.[11]

☐ African American and Latino children are less likely than White children to have a parent working full time year round: 56 percent of African American and 65 percent of Latino children versus 79 percent of White children live in families with secure parental employment.[12]

☐ Latino children (7 percent) are less likely than African American (11 percent) and White (10 percent) children to have a parent with a disability.[13]

☐ 45 percent of Latino Millennials aged eighteen to thirty-four still live with their parents.[14]

How many Latinos have never married?

☐ Of U.S-born Latina women aged fifteen to forty-four, 49 percent have never married, compared to 21 percent of Latina immigrant women.[15]

Similarly, 56 percent of U.S.-born Latino men, aged fifteen to forty-four, have never married, compared to 29 percent of immigrant Latino men.[16]

☐ 41 percent of all Latinos fifteen years of age or older have never married.[17]

How many Latinos are married? Who do they marry?

☐ In 2012, 43 percent of all Latinos fifteen years of age or older were married compared to 51 percent of Whites.[18]

☐ 60.4 percent of Latino married-couple households had children younger than eighteen present in 2012.[19]

- In nearly 50 percent of Latino married couples, both spouses work.[20]

Across the major racial and ethnic groups in the country, Latinos and Asians have the highest intermarriage rates. In a recent study, 26 percent of Latino newlyweds married a person of a different race or ethnicity as did 28 percent of Asians, compared to 9 percent of Whites and 17 percent of African Americans.[21]

- Latinos born in the United States are three times more likely to marry a non-Latino than Latino immigrants.[22]
- Unlike African Americans and Asians, there are no gender differences in intermarriage rates for Latino and White men and women newlyweds marrying outside of their race or ethnic group.[23]
- 48 percent of Latinos view the rise of interracial marriage as a change for the better, slightly more than the 43 percent of all Americans.[24]

How important is being married and having children to Latinos?

- Slightly more young Latinos (sixteen to twenty-five years old) place a higher value on being married than the overall adult American population: 56 percent versus 53 percent.[25]
- A larger gap exists between young Latinos and the general public regarding being a parent: 70 percent versus 61 percent.[26]

What is the divorce rate among Latinos?

- In 2012, 8.5 percent of Latinos fifteen years of age or older were divorced, compared to 11.5 percent of Whites and 12.2 percent of African Americans.[27]
- Of divorced Latinos, 46.5 percent are between the ages of fifty and seventy-four.[28]

How many Latinos are in non-married partnerships?

Latina women held the highest rate of cohabiting in the United States at 16 percent, compared to 11 percent of White women and around 9 percent of African American women.[29]

- There are 1.7 million unmarried couples living together where at least one member of the couple is Latino; in almost 60 percent of those couples, both members are Latino.[30]

What can we learn about Latino dating trends from the Facebook dating app *Are You Interested?*

- Latina women are more likely to respond to White men who contact them through *Are You Interested?* than to men of any other race, as are women of all other races/ethnicities except for African American women.
- On the other hand, Latino men are more likely to respond to Asian women who contact them. This is true of men of all other races/ethnicities except for Asian men, who are more likely to respond to Latina women who contact them.[31]

What childcare role do grandparents play in Latino families?

53 percent of Latino grandparents provide some form of non-residential care, such as babysitting, of their grandchildren.[32]

- Around 20 percent or 540,000 grandparents who are primary caregivers to their grandchildren are Latino.[33]
- 31 percent of Latino grandparents co-living with their grandchildren are the primary caregivers to their grandchildren.[34]
- 56 percent of children whose primary caretaker is a grandparent also live with one of their parents.[35]

How many Latino children are in foster care?

◻ Only 24 percent of Latino children with no living parents are in foster care. The majority live with grandparents, other family members, or a mix of relatives and non-relatives.[36]

◻ In February 2013, 20,654 of the 35,109 children under the supervision of the Los Angeles County Department of Children and Family Services were Latino—almost 59 percent of all the children under their supervision.[37]

◻ In California, "Latino children with U.S.-born mothers were referred, substantiated, and entered foster care at roughly 1.55 times the rate of White children," while Latino children of immigrant mothers entered foster care at half the rate of White children.[38]

How many Latino children are adopted and how many adoptive parents are Latino?

◻ Of the 74,000 adopted children in the United States in 2006, 111,000 or 5 percent were Latino.[39]

◻ Latino parents account for only 5 percent of parents who adopt through the foster care system and 7 percent of parents who adopt domestically via private organizations.[40]

RELIGION

What are the primary religious affiliations of Latinos?

◻ Just over half (53 percent) of Latinos identify as Catholic, 12 percent mainline Protestant, 13 percent "born again" or evangelical Protestants, 6 percent with a non-Christian religion, and 12 percent are unaffiliated.[41]

Current data reveal that 20 percent of Latinos who were raised Catholic leave the church.[42]

> **While 13 percent of Latinos are evangelical Protestants, only 7 percent were raised in that religion.**[43]

- Almost one-in-ten Latino immigrants is not affiliated with any organized religion, compared to 20 percent of all Latinos. Slightly more third-generation Latinos (24 percent) report they are unaffiliated.[44]
- One third of Latinos attend church weekly or more often, with just shy of two-thirds of Evangelicals reporting they attend church with this frequency.[45]

NEIGHBORHOODS

Do most Latinos live in segregated neighborhoods?

- Some 91 percent of Latinos in the United States live in metropolitan areas.[46]
- The average or "typical" Latino, lives in a neighborhood that is 45 percent Latino, even though Latinos represent just 17 percent of the total population.[47]
- Similarly, the "typical" African American lives in a neighborhood that is 45 percent African American, though African Americans represent only 12 percent of the total population.[48]
- Dominicans suffer the highest levels of residential segregation of all Latino groups, followed by Central Americans. South Americans experience the lowest levels of segregation among Latinos, while Mexicans, Puerto Ricans, and Cubans occupy the middle ground between lowest and highest.[49]
- Between 1990 and 2010, residential segregation decreased for every Latino national origin group except Mexicans.[50]

Do most Latinos live in lower income neighborhoods?

- In 2010, the average Latino lived in a neighborhood with a median income that was almost a quarter less than the median income in neighborhoods where most Whites live.[51]

□ The typical Dominican lived in a neighborhood with a median income nearly a third less than the median income in neighborhoods where most Whites live, while most South Americans lived in neighborhoods with a median income nearly on a par with where most Whites live.[52]

□ On average, between 1990 and 2009, affluent Latinos were more likely to live in neighborhoods with fewer resources than poor Whites.[53]

FREE TIME AND DAILY ACTIVITIES

What leisure and daily activities are important to Latinos?

□ Stereotypes aside, cooking and eating are some of Latinos' favorite activities: Latino millennials, for example, are slightly more likely than non-Latinos to say they really enjoy cooking, 50 percent compared to 47 percent. Only 20 percent of Latinos report eating store-made meals, compared to 29 percent of non-Latino millennials.[54]

□ Of the Latino population, 86 percent like to see a movie at a theater as a way to spend time with their friends and family, and 66 percent enjoy discussing the movie afterwards.[55]

□ In a 2012 survey, Latino Millennials aged eighteen to twenty-nine reported on what they do in their free time:

   ▪ **Spend time with family:** Millennials living with their parents spend 21 percent of their time with family, and those who live on their own commit 31 percent of their time with family.

   ▪ **"Me time":** Latinos who live on their own or have their own family spend 14 percent of their time on "me time," slightly more than non-Latinos (10 percent).

- **Friends:** Millennial Latinos spend between 12 to 13 percent of their time with their friends.[56]
- According to the most recent data available, 68 percent of Latino children are read to three or more times per week, a smaller share than that of White (91 percent) and African American (78 percent) children.[57]

How satisfied and optimistic are Latinos?

- Around 87 percent of Latinos report that they are "satisfied" or "somewhat satisfied" with their lives, a 6 percent increased from 2008. African Americans and Whites reported similar levels to Latinos.[58]
- Of the Latino population, 73 percent agree that, "The way things are in America, people like me and my family have a good chance of improving our standard of living," an increase from 2008, and 27 percentage points higher than Whites (46 percent), and slightly higher than African Americans (71 percent).[59]

Until we get equality in education, we won't have an equal society.

—*Supreme Court Justice Sonia Sotomayor*

Today, one in four children enrolled in U.S. public schools is Latino. Latino children face a daunting and too familiar reality in the public education system: under-resourced schools in impoverished and often segregated neighborhoods and below average standardized test scores. But Latino students are increasingly beating the odds. While they still suffer higher dropout rates than any other racial or ethnic group, the gap is closing dramatically and college enrollment is up. In 2012, for the first time, Latino high school graduates were more likely to enroll in college than Whites. And in the past four decades, the number of Latinos who received college degrees increased by 700 percent. Latino students enjoy the support of their parents, who attend parent-teacher conferences and check their children's homework all the way through high school. Despite some uplifting shifts, it is still hard to ignore the bleak indicators of underserving public schools. Yet, with education as the number one concern for Latino voters, this growing and increasingly better-educated electorate has the power to insist that we mend the American education system.

SNAP STATS

In line with the total U.S. adult population, a high school degree is the highest level of education completed by nearly a third of Latinos. However, Latinos trail behind the total population when it comes to higher education. While more than half of American adults have some college or hold an undergraduate or graduate degree, only a third of Latinos do.

The number of Latino students, already a sizable portion of the public school population, is growing rapidly, while the White student population shrinks. Currently, over 12.4 million U.S. public school students are Latino. In little over twenty years, one-in-three public school children will be Latino.

Most Latino public school students attend segregated schools in neighborhoods with above average poverty and crime rates. Often taught by non-Latino teachers new to the field, Latino students overwhelmingly underperform on standardized tests. Their schools' increasingly challenged "Zero Tolerance" disciplinary policies lead to high expulsion and arrest rates, too often exiling Latinos and other students of color to the criminal justice system.

As the Latino high school dropout rate decreases, college enrollment is rising. Latinos drop out of high school at twice the rate of their African American classmates and at four times the rate of White students. Happily, the Latino dropout rate decreased by nearly 50 percent in the last 25 years and almost half of those completing high school are enrolling in college. Latinos are now the largest ethnic/racial minority on U.S. college campuses.

Latino parents' concern and involvement in their children's education contributes to these rising educational attainment rates. Education was the top priority for Latino voters in the 2012 elections. Just like other American parents, the majority of Latino parents attends parent-teacher conferences and checks their children's homework.

What is the highest level of education completed by Latino adults in the United States?

- Of the over 35 million Latinos eighteen years and older in the United States in 2013, almost a third (11 million) only completed high school, placing them at a comparable level to the total adult U.S. population.[1]
- Nearly 6 million Latino adults have some college but no degree, 2.4 million hold an associate's degree, almost 3.4 million have a bachelor's degree, and 1.4 million completed advanced degrees. While more than a third of Latinos have some college or an undergraduate or graduate college degree, this is significantly less than the 57 percent of the total U.S. adult population.[2]
- Only 1.7 million Latino adults completed just ninth grade, while 5.8 million (16.5 percent) have not.[3]
- A third of Latino immigrants have less than a ninth grade education.[4]

How many Latino children are enrolled in the nation's public schools?

- About one out of four public school students is Latino.[5]
- In 2011, over 12.4 million Latinos were enrolled in U.S. public schools, pre-K through twelfth grade, compared to 27.4 million White, 8.3 million African American, and 2.3 million Asian American children.[6]
- By 2036, one out of three public school (pre-K–12) students will be Latino and the share of White students will continue to decrease.[7]

How many Latino children are in nursery school?

- Of public nursery school students, 26 percent are Latino.[8]

- About 760,000 Latino children are in public nursery schools, compared to about 1.3 million White, 562,000 African American, and only 120,000 Asian American.[9]

How many Latino children are in public elementary schools?

One-quarter of students in public elementary schools are Latino.[10]

- There are 7.4 million Latino, 15.7 million White, 4.7 million African American, and 1.3 million Asian-American children in public elementary schools.[11]
- Almost 1 million Latino children are in public kindergartens, compared to 1.9 million White, about 500 thousand African American, and less than 200 thousand Asian American children.[12]

How many Latino elementary school children are held back a grade?

- In 2009, 10 percent of Latina girls and 20 percent of Latino boys in the ninth grade had ever been held back a grade.[13]
- Fewer Asian American girls (3 percent) and boys (4 percent) and White girls (8 percent) and boys (11 percent) were held back, but more African American girls (21 percent) and boys (29 percent) were held back.[14]

How many public high school students are Latino?

- More than one out of five public high school students is Latino.[15]
- There are 3.3 million Latinos, 8.5 million Whites, 2.5 million African Americans, and 635,000 Asian Americans in public high schools.[16]

What is the Latino high school dropout rate?

- The high school dropout rate for Latinos is 14 percent, almost three times the White high school drop-

out rate and twice the rate for African Americans
(7 percent).[17]

While still too high, the Latino dropout rate dropped dramatically from 32 percent in 1990 to its current 14 percent rate, a much
sharper decline than in either the White or African American
communities.[18]

- 76 percent of Latinos aged 18 to 24 have a high
  school diploma or General Education Development
  (GED) degree, and almost half of them are enrolled in
  two- and four-year colleges.[19]
- Between 1990 and 2012, the educational attainment rate of twenty-five to twenty-nine year olds
  who received at least a high school diploma or its
  equivalent increased for Latinos from 58 percent to
  75 percent. The gap between Whites and Latinos
  with high school diplomas narrowed from 32 to
  20 percentage points.[20]

How many Latino high school students work after school?

- In 2010, 12 percent of Latino high school students
  age sixteen and older were employed, with 21 percent of these working twenty hours a week or
  more.[21]
- Fewer Latino high school students were employed
  than White (22 percent), but slightly more than
  African American (11 percent) or Asian American
  (8 percent) students.[22]

How many Latinos are enrolled in private school?

- Of the 500 thousand Latinos enrolled in private
  schools, grades K–12, 60 percent attended Catholic
  schools.[23]

How many Latinos attend college?

- In 2012, for the first time more Latinos who

graduated from high school enrolled in college than Whites who graduated that year.

- A record-breaking 16.5 percent of all U.S. college students aged eighteen to twenty-four years old in 2011 were Latino.[24]
- Nearly half (45.6 percent) of Latinos aged eighteen to twenty-four years old with a high school diploma enroll in a two- or four-year college.[25]
- Of the 12.7 million college students in the United States, over 2 million were Latino, 7.9 million White, 1.6 million African American, and 748,000 Asian American.[26]

Latinos are the fastest growing college population with a growth rate of 15 percent between 2010 and 2011. While the number of White college students also grew during this time period (only by 3 percent), the numbers of African American students decreased by 3 percent and Asians by 8 percent.[27]

- Of the 2 million Latinos enrolled in college (ages eighteen to twenty-four years old), more than half—1.2 million—were enrolled in four-year colleges and universities in 2011.[28]
- Latinos are the largest ethnic/racial minority group on college campuses. Of all students between eighteen and twenty-four years old, 13 percent of those in four-year colleges and 25 percent of those in two-year colleges are Latino.[29]

How many Latinos are awarded college and advanced degrees?

- Over the past four decades, the numbers of Latinos receiving college degrees (associate's and bachelor's) grew by sevenfold.[30]
- While that growth rate outpaces Whites and African Americans, Latinos haven't caught up yet. Of the 1.7 million bachelor's degrees awarded in 2010,

only 140,000 went to Latinos. Whites were awarded 1.2 million bachelor's degrees that year, and African Americans were awarded 165,000 bachelor's degrees.[31]

□ At the associate's level, the 112,000 degrees awarded to Latinos almost closed the gap with African Americans (114,000), but still lagged far behind Whites (553,000).[32]

□ Latina women were awarded a larger share of bachelor's (61 percent) and associate's degrees (62 percent) than Latino men.[33]

□ In 2010 about 44,000 Latinos were awarded master's degrees, still a small number, but more than twice the number of master's degrees awarded to Latinos ten years earlier. Of all master's degrees awarded, Whites received 73 percent, African Americans 13 percent, and Asian Americans and Latinos 7 percent each.[34]

□ Just 8,000 Latinos, 10,000 African Americans, and close to 17,000 Asians received doctoral degrees in 2010, compared to 104,000 Whites.[35]

Do most Latino students attend segregated public schools?

Almost half (43 percent) of Latino and 38 percent of African American children attend "intensely segregated schools" with 10 percent or less White students enrolled. A full 80 percent of Latino and 74 percent of African American students attend schools with 50 percent or less White students.[36]

□ 14 percent of Latino children attend "apartheid" schools with an enrollment of 1 percent or less White children.[37]

□ The typical Latino student attends schools "with almost double the share of low-income students" than schools attended by typical White or Asian students.[38]

How many Latino children participate in bilingual education and ESL programs in U.S. schools?

- In 2010, almost 3.6 million Latino students in U.S. schools were classified as "English Language Learners," (ELL) entitled to participate in English language acquisition programs, such as English as a Second Language, bilingual, or English-language immersion.[39]

- Spanish was the most common primary language spoken by English Language Learners in U.S. schools across 44 states.[40] Only 35 percent of English Language Learners, over 70 percent of whom are Latino, are reading at or above U.S. Department of Education established proficiency levels.[41]

- Standardized reading tests in the fourth and eighth grades reveal a persistent "achievement gap" between students in ELL programs and "mainstream" students.[42]

How many Latino students with disabilities are enrolled in U.S. schools?

- Of students with disabilities receiving services under IDEA (Individuals with Disabilities Education Act), 20 percent are Latino, 21 percent are African Americans, and 54 percent are White.[43]

How well do Latino elementary school students perform on standardized tests of academic achievement in reading, mathematics, and science?

- Only 18 percent of Latinos in the fourth and eighth grades are performing at or above the reading proficiency level set by the U.S. Department of Education, compared to over 49 percent of their White peers. Only 16 percent of African American fourth graders and 14 percent African American eighth graders are performing at or above the reading proficiency level.[44]

- In the eighth grade, 20 percent of Latino students, 43 percent of White students, and 13 percent of African American students performed at or above the mathematics proficiency level.[46]
- 13 percent of Latinos in the fourth grade are performing at or above the science proficiency level set by the U.S. Department of Education, compared to over 46 percent of Whites and 10 percent of African Americans.[47]
- In the eighth grade, 16 percent of Latino students, 43 percent of White students, and 9 percent of African American students performed at or above the science proficiency level.[48]

How do Latinos' scores on the SAT compare to other American students?

- In 2011, the mean SAT critical reading score for Latinos was 451 compared to the overall average of 497 for all students.[49]
- The mean SAT mathematics score for all students was 514. Mexican student scores averaged 466, Puerto Rican students averaged 452, and for all other Latinos the average was 462.[50]
- The mean SAT writing score was 445 for Mexican Americans, 442 for Puerto Rican students, and 444 for all other Latino students. The mean score for all students taking the test that year was 489.[51]

How do school "safety measures" affect Latino students?

- A comparison of schools with a majority of students of color to predominantly White schools revealed that metal detector checks (2 percent versus 11 percent) and picture identification (3 percent versus 12 percent) were relied on more heavily in the student of color schools, while athletic drug testing was more common in the predominantly White schools (9 percent versus 5 percent).[53]
- African American (33 percent) and Latino (26 percent) students report gang activity at their schools more than White (11 percent) or Asian American (10 percent) students do.[54]
- More Latino (14 percent) and African American (16 percent) high school students report being in physical fights than White (10 percent) or Asian (6 percent) students.[55]
- One-third of Latinos report being offered illegal drugs at school, compared to 23 percent of African American, White, or Asian students.[56]
- About 9 percent of Latino and African American students report being threatened or injured with a weapon, compared to 6 percent of White and 7 percent of Asian American students.[57]
- The percentage of students subjected to hate-related name-calling does not vary significantly by race and ethnicity. A total of 10 percent of Latino, 8 percent of White, 11 percent of African American, and 9 percent of Asian American high school students report being subjected to hate-related name-calling.[58]

How are Latino students affected by school discipline practices?

- One-quarter of students suspended or expelled from school are Latino. Of all students, 39 percent of expelled students and 35 percent of suspended students are African American and a third or slightly more are White.[59]

Of students arrested in school, 37 percent are Latino, compared to 35 percent for African Americans and 21 percent for Whites.[60]

- Of students referred to law enforcement authorities by schools, 29 percent are Latino, while 42 percent are African American and 25 percent are White.[61]
- Latinos represent 42 percent of students isolated from other students as a disciplinary measure, compared to 16 percent for African Americans and 38 percent for Whites.[62]

How involved are Latino parents in their children's education?

- Similar to their White and African American counterparts, 80 percent or more of Latino parents of students in grades K-12 attend general school meetings and parent-teacher conferences.[63]
- Latino and African American parents (65 percent) are less likely to attend elementary and secondary school and class events than White parents (80 percent).[64]
- Three-quarters of Latino high school student parents check their children's homework compared to 57 percent of their White and 83 percent of their African American counterparts.[65]

How many public school teachers and principals are Latinos?

- Only 7 percent of teachers in public schools are Latino. An equal number are African American, while 83 percent are White.[66]
- Schools serving predominantly Latino and African American students are "nearly twice as likely to employ teachers who are newest to the profession."[67]
- Teachers in predominantly African American and

Latino schools earn $2,251 less annually on average than their counterparts in predominantly White schools.[68]

◻ Of the almost 90,000 principals in U.S. public schools in 2013, only 7 percent were Latino, compared to 80 percent White and 10 percent African American.[69]

Hispanics and Latinos tend to have better health than non-Hispanic Whites. . . . Hispanic cultural values such as *simpatía* (importance of displaying kindness and maintaining interpersonal harmony), *familismo* (importance of keeping warm family relationships), and *personalismo* (valuing and building warm relationships) may help to build strong social support . . . associated with better health and lower mortality risk.

—Dr. John Ruiz, Ph.D., Assistant Professor at the University of North Texas, Researcher on the Hispanic Paradox

Despite higher rates of poverty, lower employment and educational attainment, and notably less access to health care, Latinos are surprisingly hardy and healthy. They live longer than Whites and African Americans, experience an infant mortality rate equal to Whites, who are socially and economically more privileged, and enjoy lower incidences and higher survival rates for many major diseases. Referred to by researchers and media as the "Hispanic paradox," the better health of Latinos remains unexplained and unaccounted for, notwithstanding decades of research.

Equally surprising for many readers may be the depth of Latinos' support for environmental issues, such as counteracting climate change, using renewable energy, and protecting the natural environment. However, don't let the good news obscure the very real challenges faced by Latinos in accessing health care and health insurance, as well as Latinos' disproportionate exposure to pollution and contamination.

SNAP STATS

Despite the health-related hardships many Latinos face, their average life expectancy is over 80 years of age. That is more than two years longer than White Americans and six years longer than African Americans.

Latinos have the highest uninsured rate of any ethnic or racial group in the United States. Not surprisingly, almost one-quarter of Latinos do not have a regular health care provider.

Latinos have lower overall cancer rates than other Americans. They are significantly less likely than White Americans to suffer from lung cancer and have lower breast and prostate cancer rates.

Latinos are disproportionately affected by the HIV/AIDS epidemic. Latino men are three times as likely and Latina women are four times as likely as Whites to suffer from HIV/AIDS.

Latinos are much less likely to smoke than other Americans, but more likely to be obese than Whites. Obesity is an at-risk behavior that reflects more than individual decisions. Structural realities such as limited access to healthy foods play a key role. And not smoking is countered for two out of three Latinos by the fact that they live in polluted neighborhoods that fail to meet federal government air quality standards.

BY THE NUMBERS...

What is the life expectancy of Latinos?

□ Latinos' average life expectancy is over 80 years old, 2.5 years longer than White Americans and six years longer than African Americans.[1] The ethnic or racial group with the longest life expectancy in the United States is Asian American women (85.8 years).[2]

What are the leading causes of death among Latinos?

Although Latinos represented over 16 percent of the U.S. population in 2010, they accounted for only 6 percent of all deaths in the United States. Even correcting for the fact that Latinos are a younger population than Whites and African Americans does not account for Latinos' significantly lower deaths.[3]

What is the Latino infant mortality rate?

- The infant mortality rate for all Latinos is the same as it is for Whites, 5.3 per 1,000 births, and less than half the 12.4 rate for African Americans.[4]
- The infant mortality rate varies significantly among Latino national origin groups, ranging from 4.0 per 1,000 live births for Mexicans to 4.5 for Central and South Americans to a significantly higher 7.2 for Puerto Ricans.[5]

Do Latinos have a harder time accessing healthcare?

Almost a quarter of Latinos do not have a regular health care provider. Latinos are twice as likely African Americans and three times as likely as Whites to lack a regular healthcare provider.[6]

- Access is even more limited among the many uninsured Latinos: almost a third do not have a regular healthcare provider.[7]
- Latinos have the highest uninsured rate of any ethnic or racial group in the United States. Almost 40 percent of Mexicans, 52 percent of Puerto Ricans and Cubans, and 46 percent of other groups are uninsured.[8]

Figure 7.1. Top Ten Causes of Death Among Hispanics

1. Cancer	6. Chronic Liver Disease and Cirrhosis
2. Heart Disease	7. Chronic Lower Respiratory Diseases
3. Accidents	8. Influenza and Pneumonia
4. Stroke	9. Homicide
5. Diabetes	10. Kidney Disease

Source: Office of Minority Health and Health Equity, "10 Leading Cases of Death for Hispanic/Latinos in 2009," U.S. Centers for Disease Control and Prevention, July 2, 2013, www.cdc.gov/minorityhealth/populations/REMP/hispanic.html#10.

- Almost half of immigrants who have been in the United States for less than five years do not have a regular healthcare provider.[9]
- For the one in three Latinos who do not speak English well, language is another barrier to health care. Almost one third of them do not have a regular healthcare provider.[10]
- A majority of Americans (51 percent) are unaware of the impact of ethnic and racial disparities on Latino access to health care.[11]

Are recognized health risk factors more prevalent among Latinos?

Obesity and Overweight

- Adult Latinos are 20 percent more likely than adult Whites to be obese and 10 percent less likely than African Americans.[12]
- Close to one out of three adult Latinos is obese.[13]
- White men are more likely to be obese than White women, but for Latinos it is the other way around:

Latina women are more likely to be obese than Latino men.[14]

□ Of Mexican women, 78 percent are obese or overweight compared to 60 percent of White women.[15]

Smoking

□ Latino men are 30 percent less likely to smoke than White and African American men.[16]

Latinas are about 50 percent less likely to smoke than both White and African American women.[17]

Do Latinos have the same access to healthy foods as other Americans?

□ Latino neighborhoods have only 32 percent as many supermarkets as non-Latino neighborhoods, limiting Latino families' access to retailers more likely to offer healthy food at affordable prices.[18]

□ Latino families are more likely than White families to live in neighborhoods with fewer supermarkets offering a full range of healthy food and to depend more on small neighborhood stores that do not.[19]

□ Latinos are also less likely to have access to a car than Whites and more likely to depend on public transportation that limits both how often they can shop and how much food they can transport.[20]

Do Latinos suffer from major diseases at the same rate as other Americans?

Cancer

□ Latina women and men have lower overall cancer rates than Whites: Latinos are half as likely to suffer from lung cancer, Latina women are 30 percent less likely to suffer from breast cancer as White women, and Latino men are 20 percent less likely to have prostate cancer than their White counterparts.[21]

- On the other hand, Latino men and women have significantly higher rates of stomach and liver cancer than Whites and are more likely to die from these forms of cancer.[22]
- Latina women are almost twice as likely to have cervical cancer and more likely to die from it.[23]

Heart Disease and Hypertension

Latinos are 20 percent less likely to suffer from heart disease and 30 percent less likely to die as a result of heart disease than Whites and African Americans.[24]

- Latinos are 10 percent less likely than Whites to suffer from hypertension and more than 40 percent less likely than African Americans.[25]

Stroke

- While Latinos suffer strokes at about the same rate as Whites, Latinos are 20 percent less likely to die as a result of strokes.[26]
- Like Whites, Latinos are 60 percent less likely to have strokes than African Americans.[27]

Diabetes

Latino adults are almost twice as likely than Whites to suffer from diabetes.[28]

- Latino adults with diabetes are 1.5 times as likely as Whites to die as a result of the disease.[29]

Asthma

- In 2011, 3.6 million Latinos reported that they currently had asthma.[30]
- The incidence of asthma is slightly lower for all Latinos than it is for Whites.[31]
- Puerto Ricans, however, are twice as likely as other

Latinos and Whites to have asthma and more likely to die from the disease.[32]

HIV/AIDS

□ Latinos accounted for 20 percent of all HIV infection cases in 2011.[33]

□ Latino men are three times as likely to have either HIV infection or AIDS as White men, compared to African American men, who are more than seven times as likely as White men.[34]

□ Latinas were four times as likely to have AIDS in 2011 as White women, a significantly higher rate that is dwarfed by that of African American women who are twenty-three times as likely as White women to have AIDS.[35]

□ Latino men are 2.5 times as likely as White men to die of HIV/AIDS, compared to African American men, who are seven times as likely to die from the disease as White men.[36]

□ Latinas are twice as likely as White women to die of HIV/AIDS, compared to African American women who are fifteen times more likely to die of HIV than White women.[37]

Are many Latinos living with disabilities?

□ The U.S. Census Bureau estimates a slightly lower incidence of disability among Latinos (8.5 percent) compared to Whites (13.1 percent).[38]

How are Latinos affected by sexually transmitted diseases?

□ Latinos are twice as likely as Whites to contract gon-orrhea and syphilis.[39]

□ Latinos are three times as likely as Whites to be in-fected by chlamydia.[40]

Do Latino sexual behaviors differ from other Americans?

□ Among women fifteen to forty-four years old, 88 percent of Latinas, 82.9 percent of White, and

- 80.8 percent of African American women are sexually active with men.[41]
- Among men fifteen to forty-four years old, 84.5 percent of Latino men are sexually active with women, compared to 82 percent of White men and 86.1 percent of African American men.[42]
- Fewer Latino women between fifteen and forty-four years of age (6.3 percent) report having sex with other women than White (14.8 percent) or African American (11.3 percent) women.[43]
- Among men fifteen to forty-four years old, 3.8 percent of Latinos, 6 percent of Whites, and 2.4 percent of African Americans report having sex with another man.[44]
- About one in three Latino high school students is sexually active. Fewer Latina girls (31.6 percent) are sexually active than Latino boys (35.3 percent). African American boys (46 percent) and girls (39.6 percent) and White girls (35 percent) are more likely to be sexually active than Latina girls, and slightly more Latina girls are sexually active than White boys (30 percent).[45]
- While most sexually experienced Latina women report ever having used condoms (81.9 percent), fewer of them do so than White (96.5 percent) and African American (95.7 percent) women.[46]
- More Latino men (37.5 percent) and women (27.3 percent) and African American men (47.6 percent) and women (39.4 percent) report using condoms at their last sexual encounter than White men (32.1 percent) and women (23 percent).[47]

Do Latino childbearing trends differ from other Americans?
- Of the over 3.9 million babies born in 2011, almost a quarter were Latino.[48]
- Of the 329,797 babies born to teenagers fifteen to nineteen years of age in the United States in

2011, 57 percent were born to Latinos and African Americans.[50]

> The mean age for first births for Latina women was around twenty-four in 2011, with average first birth ages ranging from around twenty-three years old for Mexican women to nearly twenty-seven years old for Cuban women.[49]

□ Birth rates for Latino teenagers (49.4 per 1,000 teenagers) were slightly higher than the rate for African American teenagers (47.4 per 1,000) and significantly higher than White teenagers (21.8 per 1,000). The decline in teenage pregnancies between 2007 and 2011, however, was also the steepest for Latinos (34 percent) compared to African Americans (24 percent) and Whites (20 percent).[51]

□ Premature births are slightly more prevalent among Latinos (11.7 percent) than Whites (10.5 percent), but significantly lower than among African Americans (17 percent).[52]

□ Twin births are less prevalent among Latinas (25 percent) than among Whites (37 percent) and African Americans (38 percent).[53]

Is contraceptive use lower among Latino women?

□ While use of birth control is higher among White women (91 percent) and African American women (86 percent), the vast majority of sexually active Latinas (81 percent) use contraceptives.[54]

□ Religious affiliation has no significant impact on the use of contraceptives among Latinas.[55]

What is the Latino abortion rate?

□ Latina women have a lower incidence of abortion

than White or African American women: Latinas accounted for 25 percent of abortions in 2010, compared to 36 percent for White women and 30 percent for African American women.[56]

Are Latino views on abortion and birth control more conservative than other Americans?

- □ Almost half of Latino adults (49 percent) believe that abortion should be legal in some or all cases compared to 59 percent of the general public.[57]
- □ There are differences of opinion on abortion between immigrant and U.S. born Latinos: more immigrant Latinos are opposed to abortion than U.S. born Latinos. In fact, support for access to abortion among second and third generation Latinos is just about 60 percent, as it is among the wider American public.[58]

A majority of Latinos supports access to birth control (60 percent), with an even higher level of support among Latina women (86 percent).[59]

- □ In a 2013 survey of over 1,000 Latino adults conducted by Planned Parenthood and the Center for Latino Adolescent and Family Health (CLAFH) at the Silver School of Social Work at New York University, respondents overwhelmingly supported comprehensive sex education in high schools.[60]

How are Latinos affected by mental illness?

- □ The rate of serious psychological distress is slightly higher among Latinos than Whites, but Whites are twice as likely as Latinos to receive treatment for it.[61]

- □ Like other immigrants, Latinos with limited English proficiency suffering from mental disorders are significantly less likely to identify a need for treatment and are more likely to go untreated longer and use fewer treatment services for mental disorders.[62]

What is the suicide rate among Latinos?

- The suicide rate among all Latino adults is half that of Whites.[63]
- The suicide rate among Latino men, while lower than Whites, is almost five times higher than among Latina women.[64]
- Yet, the prevalence of suicide attempts among Latinos in high school (10 percent) was higher than suicide attempts among African American (8.3 percent) and White (6.2 percent) students.[65]

How does alcohol and drug use among Latinos compare to other Americans?

- Government surveys found that use of alcohol or illicit drugs in the prior month was lower among Latino adults (46 percent) than other Americans (52 percent).[66]
- Binge alcohol use, however, was slightly higher among Latinos (26.3 percent) compared to the national average (24.5 percent).[67]
- Substance use varies significantly by national origin among Latinos. Puerto Ricans and Spaniards have higher rates of alcohol and illicit drug use and binge drinking than Dominicans, Mexicans, and Central Americans.[68]

How many Latino doctors and nurses are there in the United States?

- Only 5.5 percent of U.S.-educated doctors are Latino.[69]
- Under 5 percent of registered nurses are Latino.[70]

ENVIRONMENT

Are Latinos disproportionately exposed to pollution and contamination?

Approximately 66 percent of U.S. Latinos—25.6 million people—live in areas that do not meet the federal government's air quality standards.[71]

- Some 91 percent of Latinos in the United States live in metropolitan areas, where polluted air increases the risk of illness, including asthma (a disease that already affects Latinos disproportionately), and cancer.[72]
- One and a half million U.S. Latinos live in *colonias* (unincorporated communities with substandard housing) along the U.S.-Mexico border, where a lack of potable water and sewage treatment contributes to waterborne diseases such as giardiasis, hepatitis, and cholera.[73]
- More than one-third of U.S. Latinos live in western states, where arsenic, industrial chemicals, and fertilizer residues often contaminate local drinking water supplies.[74]
- The great majority (88 percent) of farmworkers are Latinos. They and their families face regular pesticide exposure, which can lead to increased risks of lymphoma, prostate cancer, and childhood cancers.[75]
- Latino children are twice as likely as White children to have higher lead blood levels associated with the risk of lead poisoning.[76]

What are Latino views on environmental issues?

- Latinos strongly favor clean energy: 83 percent believe that "coal plants and oil refineries are a thing of the past," and 86 percent "prefer that the government invest in clean, renewable energy."[77]
- While just half of all American voters believe that cli-

mate change is already happening, three quarters of Latino voters do.[78]

Over 90 percent of Latino voters embrace a "moral responsibility" to protect the wilderness and forests, the oceans, lakes and rivers and value outdoor activities like picnics, visiting parks, and the like.[79]

> The United States now has the highest incarceration rate in the world. . . . No other country in the world imprisons so many of its racial or ethnic minorities.
>
> —*Michelle Alexander*, The New Jim Crow

Nearly half of convicted federal offenders are Latinos. With so many Latinos in the criminal justice system, it is astonishing that the FBI, the agency responsible for national crime statistics, has not collected data over the years by ethnicity. Without that data, it is difficult to determine the full impact of the criminal justice system on the 53 million Latinos living in this country. Recently, in the face of criticism, the FBI announced that it would begin reporting on ethnicity in its annual Uniform Crime Report. Even with existing threads of data, it is clear that Latinos, particularly Latino men, are overrepresented in the criminal justice system, funneled out of their communities and over borders, and separated from their families. Surprisingly, Latino communities, living within walking distance of crime and drugs, and with residents frequently stopped and questioned by local and federal law enforcement, still have confidence in this justice system. Many Latinos believe that law enforcement officers actually do a good job of protecting them and that the courts treat them fairly. As more and more data surfaces, will their confidence erode?

SNAP STATS

In states with large Latino populations, Latinos have disproportionately high arrest rates. Latinos are much more likely than White Americans to get arrested and account for a disproportionate share of all felony and misdemeanor arrests. Latino children are arrested at alarming rates in states such as Texas and California.

Many Latinos live in neighborhoods where they feel unsafe. With high rates of gang participation and with homicide as a leading cause of death, more than one in three Latinos report that they live within a mile of areas that they are scared to walk in at night. Yet Latinos report being victims of violent crime and property crime, such as burglary, at lower rates.

Latinos are surprisingly confident in the criminal justice system. Despite being stopped and questioned by the police with inflated frequency, high incarceration rates, and minimal representation in law enforcement and the legal professions, many Latinos still feel that their local police do a good job enforcing the law and that U.S. courts treat Latinos fairly.

Latino men are much more likely than White men, but only half as likely as Black men, to serve time in prison. Latino boys also face high levels of incarceration, particularly in states with large Latino populations. California and Texas alone imprison the majority of incarcerated Latino youth in the United States.

Latinos account for almost half of all documented gang members in the United States. Despite these high numbers, only 3 percent of young Latinos aged sixteen to twenty-five reported that they are currently, or have been in, a gang.

Nearly half of convicted federal offenders are Latino. Almost nine out of ten Latino federal offenders were convicted of one of two offenses: immigration and/or drug trafficking related crimes. The number of federal immigration cases increased by 97 percent in the last decade.

How many Latinos are arrested?

- The FBI, the primary source for arrest data, has little information on Latino arrests. A few states, despite FBI guidelines, do track arrest information on Latinos.
- Latinos accounted for 40 percent of all felony and misdemeanor arrests in California[1] and 36 percent of all arrests in Texas, two states with large Latino populations that do track ethnicity.[2]
- In New York, Latinos are almost four times more likely than Whites to get arrested.[3]
- Of all Latinos, 15 percent say that they or someone in their immediate family has been arrested within the last five years, and nearly 25 percent of Latinos aged eighteen to twenty-nine shared this experience.[4]
- African American and Latino motorists are three times more likely to be searched than White motorists and are more likely to be ticketed.[5]

How many Latino youth are arrested?

- At a comparable rate to Whites, 25 percent of second-generation Latinos were arrested within the last year.[6]
- There are stark differences between immigrant and second-generation Latino youth offenders across the country. The crime rate of immigrant Latino youth is lower than that of second-generation youth. About 25 percent of second-generation youth have been convicted of committing a crime within the last year, compared to 17 percent of immigrant Latino youth.[7]
- Latinos make up 50 percent of all juveniles arrested in California.[8]
- The majority of Latino youth arrested in California were arrested for misdemeanor violations.[9]

How many Latinos are victimized by crime and violence?

- The rate of violent crime victimization for Latinos is 24.5 per 1,000 persons age twelve or older, slightly lower than the rate for Whites (25.2 per 1,000), and well below the rate for African Americans (34.2 per 1,000).[10]

- From 1994 to 2011 the rate of burglaries decreased by at least 50 percent across all American households. Latinos saw the greatest decline (67 percent.) from 76 to 24.9 victimizations per 1,000 households.[11]

- Homicide falls within the top ten causes of death for Latinos aged one to fifty-four. For Latinos aged fifteen to thirty-four, homicide by a firearm was the second highest cause of death after motor vehicle accidents.[12]

- Of all reported hate crimes, 7 percent target victims due to an anti-Latino bias.[13]

- Of hate crimes, 85 percent are ethnically and racially motivated.[14]

- A smaller percentage of Latinos (5 percent) and African Americans (5 percent) are victims of identity theft than Whites (7 percent). Across all ethnic groups, those with higher incomes ($75,000+) are more likely to be the victims of these crimes.[15]

What do Latinos have to say about how they are affected by crime?

- More than one in three Latinos report that there are areas within a mile of their home in which they are scared to walk home at night.[16]

- A quarter of Latinos indicated that they or an immediate family member had been questioned by the police in the previous five years.[17]

- Latino victims are less likely than Whites or African Americans to report property crime incidents such as burglary and motor vehicle theft and personal crimes such as rape and aggravated assault to the police.[18]

- Though Latinos are less likely to report crimes to

law enforcement authorities, over three-quarters of Latinos say that if they were a victim of a violent crime, they would definitely report it to the police.[19]

▫ Native-born Latinos report being victimized by a crime in the last five years at rates twice as high as immigrant Latinos.[20]

How confident are Latinos in law enforcement and the broader criminal justice system? And how do they interact with law enforcement?

▫ Six in ten native-born Latinos compared to four in ten immigrant Latinos have a fair amount of confidence that the U.S. court system will treat them fairly.[21]

▫ Six in ten of all Latinos feel confident that local police in their communities will do a good job upholding the law, particularly in dealing with gangs and gang violence.[22]

▫ 45 percent of Latinos believe that they are treated fairly by law enforcement compared to 74 percent of Whites and 37 percent of African Americans.[23]

▫ Though many Latinos are confident in their local police departments, 47 percent have very little confidence that the police will avoid using excessive force on suspects.[24]

▫ A quarter of Latinos indicated that the police had questioned them or an immediate family member in the previous five years.[25]

▫ According to the U.S. Department of Justice, overall traffic stops were a more common form of police contact with Latinos than street stops. Among African American drivers, 13 percent were stopped compared to 10 percent of Latinos and 10 percent of Whites.[26]

▫ In the first three quarters of 2013, New Yorkers were stopped and frisked 179,063 times—29 percent of those stopped were Latino and 56 percent were African American. Nearly 90 percent of those stopped were innocent.[27]

- Eight in ten Latinos believe that their local police should not be involved in identifying undocumented immigrants.[28]

How many Latinos work in law enforcement?

- Police and sheriff patrol officers are 73 percent White, nearly three times the share of Latino (13.8 percent) and African American (12.8 percent) officers combined.[29]
- Latinos account for 22 percent of local police forces serving populations over one million.[30]
- Although the FBI still primarily employs White personnel, 7 percent of FBI special agents and 5.9 percent of professional staff are Latino.[31]
- The Department of Homeland Security personnel is comprised of only 20.9 percent Latinos, although the majority of immigration-related crimes are committed along the Mexican border, which is heavily populated by Latinos. Nonetheless, the Department of Homeland Security still employs the most Latinos of any federal agency.[32]
- Though accounting for 17 percent of the national population and 95 percent of the population in border towns like Laredo, Texas, Latinos account for only 10.8 percent of all customs and border protection personnel.[33]
- In New York City, Latinos make up over 25 percent of the police force. African Americans make up 16 percent and Whites 52 percent of the force.[34]
- With 17,153 sworn officers, Puerto Rico boasts the second largest police department in the United States.[35]

How are Latinos represented in the legal profession?

- According to the U.S. Census Bureau, Latinos make up 3.4 percent of U.S. lawyers.[36]
- Latinas make up 1.04 percent of all the lawyers in the United States.[37]

- Of U.S. judges, magistrates, and judicial workers, 4.5 percent are Latino.[38]
- Of U.S. judges, magistrates, and judicial workers, 2 percent are Latina women.[39]
- Latinos make up only 7.8 percent of the justice department personnel.[40]
- In line with this trend of underrepresentation in legal professions, only 3.1 percent of law professors are Latino.[41]

What are offense and sentencing trends for Latinos?

- Though only 17 percent of the total U.S. population is Latino, over 48 percent of convicted federal offenders are Latino, significantly higher than the share of Whites (27.5 percent) and African Americans (20.4 percent).[42]
- 86 percent of Latino federal offenders were convicted of one of two federal offenses: immigration and drug trafficking related crimes.[43]
- Of the 1,341,804 prisoners serving sentences under state jurisdiction, 282,353 (21 percent) are Latino and 509,577 are African American (38 percent). The majority of Latino prisoners (57 percent) were convicted of violent crimes.[44]
- The majority of the 162,489 Latino violent crime offenders serving time in a state prison were convicted of aggravated assault (13.5 percent), murder (13.4 percent), manslaughter (13.4 percent), and rape/sexual assault (12.7 percent).[45]
- 13.6 percent of Latino prisoners under state jurisdiction are convicted of property-related crimes, with burglary accounting for 7.8 percent of all convictions.[46]

How many Latinos are in prisons and jails?

- Although Latinos are 17 percent of the U.S. population with a large share of children under eighteen, 22 percent of inmates in federal, state, and local prisons/jails are Latino.[47]

- Latino men have a one-in-six chance of facing imprisonment compared to White men's one-in-seventeen chance. Racial disparities are more severe for African American men who face a one-in-three chance of incarceration.[48]
- In 2010, the Latino male incarceration rate was more than seventeen times greater than that of Latina females; 327,200 Latino males and 18,700 Latina females were incarcerated in state and federal prisons.[49]

How many Latino youth are in prisons and jails?

- Around 22 percent of youth held in private or public residential detention facilities nationwide are Latino.[50]
- Latino youth are 40 percent more likely to be waived to adult court than White youth and are admitted to adult jails at 1.4 times the rate of Whites.[51]
- One-quarter (24 percent) of incarcerated Latino youth are held in an adult prison or jail where they face high risks of suicide and sexual abuse, significant educational disconnection, and a high likelihood of recidivism.[52]
- Latino youth are incarcerated for the following offenses:
  - 23 percent of violent offenses
  - 21 percent of property offenses
  - 26 percent of drug offenses
  - 24 percent of public order offenses
  - 26 percent of technical offenses
  - 10 percent of status offenses[53]
- California places more Latino youth in residential custody facilities than any other state in the United States. Texas comes in second with about half as many incarcerated Latino children as California. Together, the two states hold 58 percent of all incarcerated Latino youth in the country.[54]

- Around 25 percent of all juveniles in short-term juvenile detention centers are Latino, while 42 percent are African American and 32 percent are White.[55]
- Latinos account for 26 percent of youth held in long-term juvenile facilities, while 40 percent are African American and 32 percent are White.[56]

What is the impact of prison violence on Latino inmates?

- Non-heterosexual Latinos were almost twice as likely as Whites to be sexually assaulted by prison staff, 5.9 percent and 3.2 percent respectively. The rate of sexual assault on non-heterosexual African American inmates by prison staff was slightly higher (6.2 percent).[57]
- 7.5 percent of Latino incarcerated youth have been sexually assaulted by another youth or correctional facility staff member while under custody.[58]

How many Latinos are on death row or have been executed?

- Of people on death row, nearly 13 percent are Latinos, 42 percent are African Americans, and slightly more than 43 percent are White.[59]*
- Of prisoners on death row in California, 175 or 24 percent are Latino, compared to 88 prisoners or 30 percent in Texas.[60]
- Since the 1976 reinstatement of capital punishment, 1,325 people have been executed in this country. Nearly 8 percent of executed prisoners were Latino, compared to 34 percent African American and 56 percent White.[61]
- Of the victims of all executed defendants, 76 percent

---

*Note that some states are excluded from this tabulation: Alaska, Connecticut, District of Columbia, Hawaii, Illinois, Iowa, Maine, Massachusetts, Michigan, Minnesota, New Jersey, New Mexico, New York, North Dakota, Rhode Island, Vermont, West Virginia, and Wisconsin. [Connecticut and New Mexico repealed the death penalty prospectively. The men already sentenced in each state remain under sentence of death.]

were White, 15 percent were African American, and 6 percent were Latino. Of White defendants' victims, 94 percent were White; 34 percent of African American defendants' victims were African American and 60 percent were White; and 54 percent of Latino defendants' victims were Latino and 44 percent White.[62]

What portion of people arrested and convicted of drug-related offenses are Latino?

□ Around 16 percent of Latino prisoners under state jurisdiction were convicted of drug related crimes, compared to 18 percent of African Americans and 14 percent of Whites.[63]

□ Latinos accounted for over 45 percent of Drug Enforcement Administration (DEA) federal arrests, compared to only 26 percent for Whites and 25 percent for African Americans.[64]

□ Over 45 percent of drug offenders convicted and sentenced in federal court are Latino, 25.9 percent are African American, and 25.3 percent are White.[65]

□ Though Latinos account for a majority of drug-related federal sentences, African Americans account for more than 85 percent of crack cocaine–related federal sentences, while Whites made up 48 percent of methamphetamine offenders. Crack cocaine defendants are sentenced on average to 78 months compared to cannabis offenders (65 percent Latino) who serve less than a third of that time.[66]

How active are Latinos in gangs?

□ Latinos account for almost half (46 percent) of all documented gang members in the United States. African Americans make up 35 percent, and only 11 percent are White.[67]

□ Despite the high numbers of documented Latino gang members, only 3 percent of young Latinos aged sixteen to twenty-five report that they are now or have ever been in a gang.[68]

What is the impact of U.S. immigration law enforcement on Latinos?

- The number of federal immigration cases has increased by 97 percent in the last decade.[69]
- Of all individuals detained by U.S. Immigration and Customs Enforcement (ICE), 88 percent are nationals of Mexico (67 percent), Guatemala (9 percent), Honduras (6.2 percent), and El Salvador (5.5 percent).[70]
- The vast majority of immigration-related apprehensions (96 percent) occurred in southwest border states, with the largest share of apprehensions (36 percent) in Tucson, Arizona.[71]
- According to 2009 data, 94 percent of defendants accused of immigration-related federal crimes were detained prior to disposition of their cases, outpacing defendants detained for violent crimes (86.9 percent) and weapon offenses (82.3 percent).[72]
- Of individuals charged with immigration-related crimes by the federal government, 99 percent plead guilty.[73]
- Of individuals detained for immigration related offenses, 48 percent have a criminal record, about 80 percent for nonimmigration-related offenses. The majority of them are from Mexico (77 percent), Guatemala (6 percent), Honduras (6 percent), and El Salvador (5 percent)
- Immigrants with criminal records removed from the United States have been convicted of:
  - Drug related convictions (22 percent);
  - Criminal trafficking (23 percent); and
  - Immigration related offenses (20 percent).[74]

Growing up, [teen idols] were all blond, with light-colored eyes. I wanted to be that. I didn't realize how important it was to represent my background and my culture until parents of Latin descent started coming up to me. . . . Then it clicked. I can represent a different generation and a different culture.

—*Selena Gomez, actress and singer*

In the last ten years Latinos have passed a rapid succession of milestones in entertainment, technology, and sports. Latinos are increasingly watching and listening to more English language and bilingual media and entertainment. At the same time Spanish language music, television, and film are being consumed at epic rates. Yet the recent demise of the short-lived *NBC Latino* suggests that mainstream English language media is having trouble keeping its finger on the pulse of the Latino viewer. Aside from Latino-targeted English film and television, broader U.S. media depicts a rather "Latino-less" America with few onscreen speaking roles for Latino actors. When they do appear, Latinos are relentlessly typecast as objectified sirens and criminals. The picture is no better for Latinos behind the scenes: too few are television writers, executive producers, etc. This lack of fair Latino representation is mirrored in technology industry jobs.

Though Latinos still have less access to computers in their homes, the digital divide is closing. Latinos are filling the gap by relying on mobile technologies to connect with families and friends via social media and games. From Instagram and Twitter to ABC, new and traditional media are actively pursuing Latino user-bases and audiences with more talent and staff that reflect them. As these industries follow the dollar to Latino consumers' wallets, they are inevitably redefining American popular culture.

SNAP STATS

Spanish language television is flush with viewers (especially young ones) and advertising dollars. From Univision's first place ratings in the 2013 primetime "July Sweeps," to the nearly $8 billion advertisers spent on mostly Spanish language programming in 2012, the Latino viewer is a key asset for the entertainment industry.

Latino viewers are also increasingly turning to English language stations. Most Latinos get at least some of their news in English. With English language use increasing in Latino homes, bilingual programming from outlets such as *Tr3s*, *Nuvo*, and *Fusion* are showing up on screens across America.

Latinos like to see movies in theaters with friends and family. It is one of Latinos' favorite free-time activities. In 2012, Latinos bought a quarter of all movie tickets sold in the United States.

Regional Mexican is the most popular musical genre for Latinos across all ages. Hip-hop, rap, R&B, and pop are increasingly popular among young Latinos, with Beyoncé and Drake listed as some of their favorite celebrities.

From the writers' room to the screen, Latinos are overlooked in mainstream American film and television. With limited speaking roles and typecasting as criminals or gang members, gardeners, and maids, it is no surprise that Latinos are only 5 percent of broadcast television and 8 percent of cable television show creators.

Though Latinos have less access to the Internet and minimal positions within the technology industry, they are a growing and savvy user group, adopting broadband mobile technology at a greater rate than the general population. From video games to heated twitter wars, Latinos rely on technology to stay connected with friends, family, and even celebrities and professional athletes.

Latino fans enjoy sports from their country of origin, as well as typically American sports, at surprisingly similar rates. The 2012 Super Bowl was watched by 7.3 million Latinos. The enormously popular 2010 World Cup match between Argentina and Mexico was watched by 7.9 million Latinos.

BY THE NUMBERS . . .

FILMS, TELEVISION, AND RADIO

How are Latinos shaping the film industry?

- The numbers of Latinos going to see movies in theaters increased by 12 percent just between 2011 and 2012.[1]
- Though only 18 percent of moviegoers (people who have seen at least one movie in the theaters in the last year), Latinos went more often, purchasing 25 percent of all tickets bought in 2012.[2]
- The movie *Instructions Not Included* broke box office records in 2013 by bringing in $10 million in its opening weekend, the biggest opening of a Spanish language film in North America.[3]
- The 2013 English language movie *Fast and Furious 6* took in $688 million. One-third of that money, around $220 million, came from Latino moviegoers.[4]

How are Latinos shaping the television industry?

- ◻ Univision and Telemundo account for 90 percent of Spanish language television programming in the United States.[5]
- ◻ In the 2013 "July Sweeps," Univision, claiming "Numero uno is the new #1," became the first U.S. Spanish language network to top all primetime ratings for viewers in the eighteen to forty-nine age group and the coveted eighteen to thirty-four age group.[6]

In the 2012-13 season, Univision's morning talk show, *Despierta América*, reached an average of 839,000 viewers per show, an increase of 21 percent over the previous season.[7]

- • Compared to the top English language networks, *Despierta's* eighteen to forty-nine year old viewers grew by 22 percent, while ABC's *Good Morning America* didn't grow at all, *CBS This Morning* grew by just a couple of percentage points, and NBC's *Today Show* dropped by 16 percent.[8]
- • *Despierta América's* viewers are younger, with an average age of forty-four compared to ABC, CBS, and NBC's talk show viewers, whose average age was between fifty-seven and fifty-nine.[9]
- • *Despierta's* advertising revenue grew by a dramatic 52 percent to $163 million from the previous season.[10]
- ◻ Univision's novella, *Amores Verdaderos*, outperforms English language primetime competition regularly.[11]
- ◻ According to a UCLA study on Latino stereotypes in the media, Fox News audiences are more likely to agree that Latinos are on welfare (56 percent), take jobs from Americans (43 percent), and have too many children (42 percent) than ABC, NBC, CBS, and MSNBC audiences.[12]

How do Latinos keep up with the news?

- Around 80 percent of Latino adults stated they kept up with the news "a lot," or "some."[13]

In 2012, 82 percent of Latino adults said they get at least some of their news in English.[14]

- The number of Latinos who get the news exclusively in English increased from 22 percent to one-third between 2006 and 2012.[15]
- The number of Latinos who say they get the news exclusively in Spanish slipped from 22 percent to 18 percent between 2006 and 2012.[16]
- 86 percent of Latinos get the news on a typical weekday from network, local, or cable television news.[17]
- Just over 40 percent of Latinos get the news from print media.[18]
- On average Latinos spend close to fifty minutes a day reading the newspaper.[19]
- 70 percent of U.S.-born Latino adults get the news on the Internet.[20]
- Only 30 percent of Latinos who get the news exclusively in Spanish get the news from print media. Meanwhile, 93 percent of them say they get the news on a typical weekday from Spanish language television.[21]
- Of all Latinos, 56 percent say that they get the news on a typical week day from radio; 61 percent of bilingual Latinos and 58 percent of all Latinos aged eighteen to forty-nine get the news from the radio.[22]
- 78 percent of Latinos aged eighteen to twenty-nine and 76 percent of Latino's earning over $50,000 a year get the news on a typical weekday on the Internet.[23]

What are Latinos watching on television?

- On average, Latinos watch nearly twenty-seven hours a week of traditional television, and about two hours a week of time-shifted programming (DVR, etc.).[24]
- The amount of Latinos watching time-shifted television (DVR, etc.) increased by more than 20 percent from 2012 to 2013.[25]
- Latinos over thirty-five years old watch more television than Latinos between the ages of twelve and thirty-five.[26]
- *The Voice* followed by *The Big Bang Theory, Modern Family*, and *American Idol* are the most popular English language network television shows among Latino viewers.[27]
- Univision, the leading Spanish language network, aired the ten top-rated Spanish language primetime programs. *Amores Verdaderos*, a nightly telenovela, was in the top five.[28]
- Nearly a third of all predominantly English-speaking Latinos spend more than an hour a day watching Spanish language television.[29]

Latinos are more likely to watch television with a family member or friend than the general public. Latinos co-viewed 59 percent of all primetime Spanish language programming while the general market co-viewed only 48 percent of English language programming.[30]

Is radio still relevant to the Latino population?

- 94 percent of Latinos listen to the radio, compared to 92 percent of African Americans and 90 percent of the general public.[31]
- On average, Latinos listen to the radio around sixty hours a month, nearly two hours a day, at comparable rates to Whites and African Americans.[32]

- Latino adults are 89 percent more likely than the average adult to listen to Spanish radio programming.[33]

Who are the top Latino celebrities in the U.S.?

- Latinos are 18 percent more likely than the general U.S. population to follow a celebrity on social media.[34]
- Beyoncé, Drake, Jennifer Lopez, Shakira, Jenni Rivera, Marc Anthony, Pitbull, Selena, Romeo Santos, and Daddy Yankee are the top ten favorite music celebrities among Latinos aged eighteen to thirty-four.[35]

In 2012, Jennifer Lopez was ranked the #1 most powerful celebrity of the year by _Forbes Magazine_.[36]

- Latinos Jennifer Lopez, George Lopez, Sofia Vergara, and Charlie Sheen all made the _Forbes_ 2013 Top 100 Most Powerful Celebrities list.[37]
- From starring in one of the top rated and awarded shows in America to a bounty of endorsement deals, for the second year in a row, Colombian-born Sophia Vergara is television's top earning actress, earning close to $30 million in 2013 alone.[38]

How many Latinos are producers and directors in film and television?

- Nearly 6,000 Latino producers and directors were employed in the United States in 2012, accounting for just under 5 percent for all producers and directors.[39]
- In 2012, 13,608 Latino broadcast and sound engineering technicians and radio operators made-up 12.5 percent of all employed members of that group in the United States.[40]
- According to a UCLA study, in the 2011–12 television

season, 5 percent of the 112 broadcast television show creators and 8 percent of 206 of cable television programming creators were people of color.[41]

How many Latinos work in other "behind the scenes" professions?

- About 6,000 of the 57,000 employed television, video, and motion picture camera operators and editors were Latino (10.7 percent) in 2012.[42]

According to the Writer's Guild of America, in the 2011–12 season only 4 percent of the 1,722 union writers working on 190 broadcast and cable English language television shows were Latino.[43]

- Around 80 percent, or fifty-three of the sixty-five Latino union members writing for broadcast and television are working on dramas.[44]

How do Latino actors fare in film, television, and theater?

Latinos held a meager 4.2 percent of speaking roles in the five hundred top grossing films from 2007–12.[45]

- The top three roles Latinos played in the television and film were criminal or gang member, gardener or landscaper, and maid or housekeeper.[46]
- A USC study evaluating five hundred top grossing films from 2007–12 found that Latino women are the demographic most likely to be shown in nude or sexy attire. Latino men are more likely to be depicted as father figures and relational figures than other men of color.[47]

How many Latinos have won Oscars, Emmys, Grammys and Tonys?

- Fourteen U.S.-born Latinos have been nominated for an Academy Award; of those, four won the award.

Jose Ferrer, the first Latino to win the award, in 1950, is the only U.S.-born Latino to win a leading role award.[48]

Rita Moreno was the first and is still the only Latina to have won an Oscar, an Emmy, a Grammy, and a Tony award.[49]

- Only six other Latinos have won major Emmy Awards since the 1970s: Ricardo Montalban (1978), Edward James Olmos (1985), Jimmy Smits (1990), John Leguizamo (1999), Kenny Ortega (choreography, 2006), and America Ferrera (2007).[50]
- Since 1990 only four Latinos won major Golden Globe Awards: Andy García (1990), Jimmy Smits (1995), Benicio Del Toro (2000), and America Ferrera (2007).[51]
- For Latino adult viewers, the 2012 Latin Grammys were more popular than the Academy Awards, the Golden Globe Awards and the primetime Emmy Awards.[52]
- The 14th annual Latin Grammy Awards in 2013 reached just under 10 million viewers and boosted Univision's ratings to the evening's third most watched primetime television network among adults eighteen to forty-nine, and second among those aged eighteen to thirty-four.[53] The tag "@LatinGrammys" was the evening's most mentioned program account across all of Twitter TV.[54]
- The Latin Grammys boosted Univision's ratings that evening to the #1 watched primetime network for adults aged eighteen to forty-nine in markets located in Latino hot spots such as: Los Angeles, Miami, Houston, Dallas, Phoenix, and Sacramento.[55]

TECHNOLOGY

Do many Latinos work in the technology industry?

- Latinos hold fewer than 7 percent of the jobs in the

Science, Technology, Engineering, and Mathematics (STEM) occupations.[56]

◻ With only 8 percent of all STEM certificates and degrees, Latinos in the STEM workforce often hold lower-paying service positions, such as electronics and electromechanical assemblers.[57]

Though they are the ethnic and racial New Majority in California, Latinos hold just 4.2 percent of the technology jobs in the booming San Francisco Bay area, while Asians (50.1 percent) and Whites (40.7 percent) combined hold 90 percent of those positions.[58]

How do Latinos access the Internet?

◻ Of all Internet users, 10 percent are Latino.[59]
◻ In 2012, 78 percent of all Latinos reported that they use the Internet or send or receive email at least occasionally.[60]
◻ In 2012, 24 percent of Latino adults aged eighteen and older were not Internet users.[61]
◻ 62 percent of Latinos have Internet access in their home, a smaller share than the total U.S. population (72 percent).[62]
◻ Though Latinos have less Internet access, they still are an important emerging market, with home broadband usage increasing by 14 percent, more than twice the U.S. annual average.[63]
◻ According to Nielsen, the number of Latino households with tablets has increased by 45 percent from 2012 to 2013.[64]

On average, Latinos spend 8 percent more on their mobile bills than other ethnic groups.[65]

> **50 percent of Latinos use mobile devices such as smart phones and tablets to access the Internet compared to 34 percent of the general public.[66]**

- 77 percent of Latinas own smartphones.[67]

What do Latinos like to do online?

- Latinos download more music and images than any other racial or ethnic group.[68]

> **Latinos are 68 percent more likely than Whites to watch video content online and 20 percent more likely than Whites to watch video content from their mobile phones.[69]**

- According to a 2013 study by Nielsen, the top ten most searched topics for Latina women are: recipes and cooking, beauty tips, personal health and wellness, fashion advice, family health, weight/fitness, education, parenting/family advice, finances/investments, and romance/dating.[70]
- In May of 2013, Google had about 25 million unique Latino visitors, nearly 87 percent of all Latino Internet users (29.2 million).[71]
- Facebook reached 64 percent of Latino Internet users.[72]
- With its larger user base, Facebook reaches a higher number of Latinos than Instagram or Twitter. However, Latinos account for 20 percent of Instagram's user base compared to 14 percent of Facebook's and 12 percent of Twitter's user base.[73]
- Latinos, in general, tweet more than any other group, and on Facebook they "like" posts, comment, and upload photos more than other users.[74]
- While watching television, Latinos are 50 percent more likely than non-Latino viewers to interact with

social media related to television across genres, with sports programming leading the ratings.[75]

What are some video game trends among Latinos?

▢ On average, Latinos aged under thirty-four spend around forty minutes a day playing video games on a console. Latino children aged twelve to seventeen are more likely than any other Latino age group to play video games on a console, averaging nearly an hour a day of play time.[76]

▢ Latino adults are 45 percent more likely than the average adult Internet user to have purchased simulation gaming software for home use within the last year.[77]

▢ Latinos are 43 percent more likely than the average adult Internet user to have purchased an action and adventure video game within the last year.[78]

▢ Latinos like to game with friends and family. They are 42 percent more likely than the average adult Internet user to have played multiplayer console games online within the last thirty days.[79]

MUSIC

What are key music listening and purchasing trends among Latinos?

▢ Regional Mexican is the most popular genre of music for about 20 percent of Latino radio listeners twelve and older. Spanish contemporary/Spanish hot contemporary, the second most popular genre, garners almost 11 percent.[80]

▢ Regional Mexican is also the top music genre for 42 percent of Latinos eighteen to thirty-four. For Latinos over thirty-five, salsa/merengue (40 percent) and Latin ballads/romantic (39 percent) are the top genres.[81]

▢ Hip-hop, rap, R&B, and pop are the other genres

in the top ten for those aged eighteen to thirty-four but do not make the top ten list for those over thirty-five.[82]

- Pop contemporary hit radio (Pop CHR), which ranks third among all audiences, is also highly ranked among Latino radio listeners. Reaching nearly 10 percent of all Latino listeners, Pop CHR is most popular among Latina women, especially those who primarily speak English.[83]

- In the past three years the number of Latin music track downloads rose from 31.1 million in 2010 to 33.7 million in 2011 and 35.3 million in 2012.[84]

- Of the Latin music albums purchased in 2012, 86 percent were in the CD format, while only 14 percent were bought digitally.[85]

Over one in four Latinos listened to music via the online music platform Pandora in 2012, doubling the number of Latino listeners in just one year,.[86]

- Of adult Latino music listeners, 56 percent are female.[87]

LITERATURE AND BOOKS

How important are books and literature to the Latino population?

- On average, Latinos sixteen and older read eleven books a year, compared to Whites who read an average of nineteen books and African Americans who read an average of twelve books annually. [88]

- Latino children read an average of fourteen minutes more a day than White children.[89]

- Of readers who read via an e-reader, 23 percent are Latino, while 29 percent are White and 22 percent are African American.[90]

- Spanish language books sales make up 10 percent of the total U.S. market.[91]
- According to Pedro Huerta, Director of Kindle content at Amazon, 77 percent of all Spanish language books published are available in the United States.[92]
- In 2013, the evangelical *Nada Que Perder (Nothing to Lose)* by Edir Macedo, sold 72,169 copies (including pre-orders that were shipped to customers) in one day at McNally Jackson Books in New York City.[93]
- In 1990, Oscar Hijuelos, author of *The Mambo Kings Play Songs of Love*, became the first Latino to win a Pulitzer Prize for fiction. In 2008, Junot Diaz became the second Latino to win the award for his work *The Brief Wondrous Life of Oscar Wao*. In 2012, Diaz went on to win a MacArthur Fellowship.[94]
- Justice Sonia Sotomayor's memoir, *My Beloved World*, debuted on the New York Times bestseller list in 2013, with sales of 38 thousand hardback books in its first week.[95]

SPORTS

What sports do Latinos watch on television?

The Super Bowl was watched by 7.3 million Latinos aged eighteen to forty-nine. Even more, 7.9 million, watched the 2010 World Cup match between Argentina and Mexico.[96]

- The Latino viewership of the Super Bowl grew by around 39 percent from 2008 to 2012.[97]
- ESPN content connects with 29 million Latino sports fans:
  - Sixty percent, or 18 million, of their Latino viewers, watch just ESPN's English language networks.
  - Twenty percent, or 5.8 million, watch the network's

English language channels and their Spanish language channel, ESPN Deportes.

- Eighteen percent, or 5.2 million, watch only ESPN Deportes.[98]

□ In May 2013, four NBA playoff games made it to the top five slots of the most watched English language cable programming by Latino viewers. The NBA conference finals brought in an average of a million Latino viewers.[99]

How many Latinos play professional sports?

□ Latinos made up 28.2 percent of all baseball players at the start of the 2013 Major League Baseball season.[100]

□ With a salary of $29 million annually, Dominican-born Alex Rodriguez of the New York Yankees was the highest paid Major League Baseball player in 2013.[101]

In 2013, Latinos were five of the top ten highest-earning players in Major League Baseball.[102]

□ Nearly a quarter of all the players in the 2013 Major League Soccer season were Latinos.[103]

□ In the 2012–13 NBA season, twenty Latino basketball players were 4.4 percent of all players in the league.[104]

□ Less than 1 percent of NFL football players are Latino.[105]

□ At the start of the 2013 Major League Baseball season, out of five managers of color, two, Manny Acta of the Cleveland Indians and Fredi Gonzalez of the Atlanta Braves, were Latino. Interestingly, Latinos make up nearly 40 percent of the league's coaching staff.[106]

□ Only the third Latino head coach in NFL history, Ron Rivera of the Carolina Panthers, is currently the only Latino head coach in the league.[107]

Are any owners and presidents of sports franchises Latinos?

□ Arturo Moreno, majority owner of the Los Angeles Angels, is one of three people of color to own a majority stake of a Major League Baseball team.[108]

□ Claudia Lezcano Del Campo of the Miami Dolphins is one of three Latinos and one of two women of color in the NFL to serve as a senior vice president.[109]

How are Latinos represented in sports media?

□ At the most widely circulated newspapers and websites in 2012, six Latinos were sports columnists, all men. Three of those six men were employed by ESPN.[110]

□ In 2012, at the highest circulating newspapers and websites five Latinos were sports editors and only one of those five was a woman.[111]

> My African roots made me what I am today. . . . They're the reason I'm from the Dominican Republic. They're the reason I exist at all.

> —*Junot Diaz, Pulitzer Prize–winning author*

The complexities of social identity are certainly no less challenging for Latinos than other Americans, and may be even more so. Identity, how we define ourselves and are viewed in relation to other people and groups, can be the source of a sense of belonging but can also spark discrimination and unconscious biases. Each of us possesses multiple, interlinked identities based on a range of characteristics, most commonly gender, ethnicity, race, sexual orientation, age, and religion. While most Latinos identify their ethnicity first by national origin, that is not the whole story of how they see themselves. They also possess a sense of "linked fate" with meaningful ties to other Latinos of different heritages. Navigating this kind of complexity also shapes how Latinos handle the construction and understanding of race. Latin American definitions of race differ and collide with U.S. definitions, leaving Latinos to reconcile the differences and possibly contribute to a new understanding of race and ethnicity in our country. The meaning and implications of gender and sexual orientation, other key aspects of identity in our society, also require adjustment as Latino views and ideas interact with different and evolving frames in the United States and across the world. This interaction between Latino and mainstream views on the many facets of identity is increasingly under examination and is proving to be integral to how all of us define ourselves.

SNAP STATS

Hispanics embrace the complexity of their ethnic identity as people of disparate national origins linked by a shared Latino fate. More than half of Latinos identify first by their family's country of origin, while almost three-fourths also believe that their "success depends on the success of other Hispanics." Most Latinos acknowledge that anti-Latino discrimination is an obstacle to that success in this country.

Nearly half of Latinos also see themselves as part of a greater whole and describe themselves as "typical Americans." An equal number believe that they "are very different from the typical American." While almost two-thirds of Latinos agree that their economic success as a group is linked to that of African Americans, almost half also appreciate that they face similar economic challenges to those of Whites.

Latinos are navigating the blurry border between race and ethnicity. When given the opportunity, most Latinos identify their race as "some other race," or volunteer "Hispanic/ Latino." More likely to marry and start families with people outside their ethnic or racial group than White or African Americans, Latinos are discovering that finding a label that fits is getting even harder.

Overall, Latinos' views of gender roles and relations are as or more egalitarian than many other Americans. Three-quarters of Latinos support the statement:"[t]oday's women's movement [is] a movement that considers the needs of men and families, too, not just women."

Contrary to media depictions of Latino homophobia, the majority of Latinos align with the majority of the American public and agree that homosexuality should be accepted rather than discouraged by society. More Latinos in the United States support same-sex marriage than oppose it.

Do Latinos think of themselves as a distinct ethnic group?

- More than half (51 percent) of Latinos identify first by their family's country of origin, e.g., Mexican, Puerto Rican, Dominican, etc.[1]
- About a quarter (24 percent) most often say "Latino" or "Hispanic" to describe themselves and just one in five (21 percent) use the term "American" first.[2]
- A solid majority of Latinos (72 percent) believe that their "success depends on the success of other Latinos/Hispanics." This sense of "linked fate" and meaningful ties to other Latinos of different nationalities is also reflected in a majority of Latinos' (61 percent) belief that undifferentiated anti-Latino discrimination is an obstacle to Latinos' success in this country.[3]

Do Latinos prefer to be called "Latino," as they are referred to in this book, or "Hispanic"?

About half of Latinos have no preference between being referred to as "Hispanic" or "Latino."

- For those that do, twice as many prefer "Hispanic" to "Latino." This is true across most origin groups, although South Americans and Central Americans in the United States are more equally divided between the two terms.[4]

How long have Latinos been in the United States?

- Latinos in the United States today trace their origins to twenty different Spanish-speaking countries, including Spain and nineteen Latin American countries.[5]
- The five-hundred–year Latino presence in the United States is longer than that of any other group except Native Americans.[6]

- Spaniards explored forty-eight of the fifty states now in the United States before the English established their first settlement.[7]
- In fact, the first European settlement in the continental United States was St. Augustine, Florida, settled by Spaniards in 1585.[8]
- Spaniards and Mexicans were already in lands annexed by the United States in the nineteenth century through wars and treaties in pursuit of the "Manifest Destiny" doctrine which increased the size of the United States by one-third. Included in annexed lands were all or parts of ten states: California, Utah, Nevada, New Mexico, Arizona, Colorado, Texas, Wyoming, Oklahoma, and Kansas.[9]
- While Spaniards and Mexicans have a longer history in the United States, in a fifty-year period from the 1930s to the 1980s waves of immigration from Latin America doubled the representation of Latinos in the United States. Today Mexicans are still the largest Latino group in our country.[10]

How diverse are the different Latino national origin groups in the United States?

- Although linked by a sense of "shared fate," Latinos are still a diverse group of twenty different national origins.[11]
- Mexicans are the youngest group with a median age of twenty-five, while Cubans are the oldest with a median age of forty years.[12]
- More Venezuelans have a college degree than other Latinos (51 percent), while only 7 percent of Salvadorans and Guatemalans do.[13]
- Argentineans are best off financially with a median annual income of $55,000, while Hondurans have the lowest median income of $31,000.[14]
- In the 2013 National Latino Survey, 39 percent of respondents agree that Latinos of different heritages have "a lot in common." An equal number (39 per-

cent) believe that Latinos share "some" values, while a small number think that Latinos of different heritages have "only a little" (15 percent) or "almost nothing" (5 percent) in common.[15]

▫ Latino views about shared values vary across different Latino groups. Fifty-one percent of Salvadorans believe that Latinos share "a lot" of values and 23 percent only "some" values. Among Puerto Ricans, 36 percent say Latinos share "a lot" of values, yet 46 percent believe that Latinos share "some" values.[16]

▫ While Latinos share a sense of identity, they also acknowledge competition with other Latinos of the same and different heritage. Depending on the country of origin, 30 percent to 40 percent note feelings of competition in education, getting jobs, and electing government officials.[17]

Do Latinos see themselves as "typical Americans"?

Nearly half of Latinos (47 percent) describe themselves as a "typical American," while an equal number (47 percent) believe that they "are very different from the typical American."[18]

▫ The majority of Latinos say that chances for "getting ahead," raising children, and treatment of the poor is better in the United States than in their home countries but also report that family ties are stronger there than here.[19]

What impact are Latinos having on American culture?

▫ According to a recent survey, a majority of non-Latinos believe that Latinos are shaping American culture. Twenty-two percent believe that Latinos have a "great deal of influence" on American culture, and another 56 percent think Latinos' influence is moderate.[20]

▫ Three-quarters of Latinos agree with non-Latinos on the influence Latinos exercise on American culture.[21]

- Nearly nine in ten non-Latinos agree that Latinos have "great" or "moderate" influence with regard to food.[22]
- About 60 percent of non-Latinos acknowledge a similar Latino influence on music and sports in the United States.[23]
- More than half of non-Lations recognize Latinos' "great" or "moderate" influence on television programming.[24]
- Forty-four percent of non-Latinos concur that Latinos have a similar influence on art in the United States.[25]

Do Latinos experience anti-Latino discrimination?

- Six out of ten Latinos agree that discrimination against Latinos is a "major problem."[26]
- Nearly four in ten (38 percent) young Latinos say they, a relative, or a close friend has been the target of ethnic or racial discrimination. This is higher than the share of older Latinos (31 percent). Also, perceptions of discrimination are more widespread among native-born (41 percent) than foreign-born (32 percent) young Latinos.[27]
- Among four possible causes of discrimination, Latinos are more likely to choose immigration status as the primary cause (36 percent), compared to skin color (21 percent), language skills (20 percent), and income and education (17 percent).[28]

Almost a quarter of Americans agree that Latinos were more often the target of discrimination than any other racial or ethnic group in the country.[29]

- How do Latinos identify racially?
- Much of the population of Latin America is racially mixed, a combination of indigenous peoples, Europeans, Africans, and Asians. In Mexico, for ex-

ample, researchers estimate that over 80 percent of the population is mixed race or *mestizo*.[30]

□ In the 2010 Census, 53 percent of Latinos identified their race as White, 2 percent as Black, and 0.7 percent as indigenous. Thirty-seven percent or 18.5 million Latinos chose "Other" and another three million (6 percent) chose "Two or more races."[31]

Yet in a 2012 survey conducted by the Pew Research Center, a little more than half (51 percent) of Latinos identified as "some other race" or volunteered "Hispanic/Latino." Just 36 percent identified as White, and only 3 percent as Black. Many Latinos simply cannot see themselves fitting U.S. racial categories.[32]

□ Many of the 2 to 3 percent Black Latinos identify with the growing and evolving "Afro-Latino" racial and ethnic category. Similarly, while their numbers are relatively small, more Latinos are identifying as indigenous or Native American Latinos.

Do Latinos believe their interests and success are tied to other racial and ethnic groups in the United States?

The extensive 2006 National Latino Survey found that most Latinos (62 percent) believe that their economic success as a group is linked to that of African Americans. First generation Latinos held that belief more strongly than Latinos of the second generation and beyond.[33]

□ About half of Latinos in the survey believed that when it comes to job opportunities, education, income, and political issues, their problems are similar to those of African Americans. More second generation and beyond Latinos saw common challenges for African Americans and Latinos than first generation Latinos do.[34]

Nearly half of Latinos agree that they face similar challenges to Whites regarding job opportunities, education, income, and political issues. With the exception of political issues, this sense of alignment is even stronger among second generation and beyond Latinos (53 percent).[35]

- Latinos are less likely to believe Asian Americans face similar problems to theirs.[36]
- While the media often focus on competition between African Americans and Latinos, two out of five Latinos don't think it exists at all, while another third believes that competition between the two groups is "weak." Only a quarter of Latinos report strong competition between African Americans and Latinos.[37]
- Fully three-quarters of all African Americans (77 percent) have a very or somewhat favorable view of Latinos, while 79 percent of Latinos have a similarly positive view of African Americans. Three-quarters of Whites also view Latinos positively and a slightly larger percentage expressed a favorable opinion of African Americans.[38]
- A majority of African Americans (70 percent), but a smaller share of Latinos (57 percent), say the groups get along very or fairly well.[39]

Are Latinos' views of gender roles more traditional than other Americans?

- Overall Latinos' views of gender roles and relations are as or more egalitarian than other Americans.[40]
- Like most Americans, a majority of Latino men and women (55 percent) believe it is "better for the family if the father works outside the home and the mother takes care of children." Yet Latino men and women worry less than the overall American public about negative impacts when both parents work outside of the home.[41]

> Generally Latino men are twice as likely as American men to assume primary responsibility for childcare, 32 percent compared to 13 percent.[42]

- More than eight in ten Latino men and women see the rise of women in the workforce as "good for society."[43]
- More than eight in ten Latino men and women support equal pay for equal work for men and women.[44]
- Latina women's aspirations for their daughters focus on "interesting work" (42 percent) over a happy marriage and children (35 percent). While Latino men place more importance on marriage and family (42 percent), almost a third value an interesting career as most important.[45]
- Three quarters of Latinos believe that "Today's women's movement is a movement that considers the needs of men and families, too, not just women."[46]
- Latinos overwhelmingly support policy changes to require employers to provide childcare benefits, paid family and medical leave, and more flexible work schedules.[47]
- Almost half of Latinos (46 percent) disagree with the more traditional view that men are better suited to political leadership than women.[48]
- A majority of Latinos support access to birth control (60 percent), with an even higher level of support among Latina women (86 percent).[49]
- Almost half of Latino adults (49 percent) believe that abortion should be legal in some or all cases, compared to 59 percent of the general public.[50]

How many Latinos are part of the LGBT community?

- About 10 percent of people in same-sex couple households are Latino.[51]

- Similar to Whites and African Americans, over 90 percent of Latinos identify as heterosexual and report being attracted only to members of the opposite sex.[52]
- About 1 percent of Latinos identify as "homosexual, gay, or lesbian" and a little more than 2 percent as bisexual.[53]
- Fewer Latina women between fifteen and forty-four years of age (6.3 percent) report having sex with other women than White (14.8 percent) or African American (11.3 percent) women.[54]
- Among men fifteen to forty-four years old, 3.8 percent of Latinos, 6 percent of Whites, and 2.4 percent of African Americans report having sex with another man.[55]
- The majority of the American public (58 percent) agrees that homosexuality should be accepted by society. As with the general public, younger Latinos and Latina women of all ages are even more accepting: two-thirds favor acceptance of homosexuality.[56]

Contrary to media depictions of Latino homophobia, 59 percent of Latinos also agree that homosexuality should be accepted rather than discouraged by society.[57]

- More Latinos in the United States support same-sex marriage (52 percent) than oppose it (34 percent). Support varies some by generation and national origin, but most notably, two-thirds of Latino Evangelicals, in line with other American Evangelicals, oppose same-sex marriage.[58]
- Demographic data on the numbers of transgender people in the United States are still rare. Estimates place the number between 0.5 percent and 2 percent of the population with 0.1 percent taking steps to transition from one gender to another.[59]
- According to an extensive survey of 6,456 trans-

gender people conducted by the National Gay and Lesbian Task Force, the combination of anti-transgender discrimination and structural racism is devastating for Latino and other transgender people of color.[60]

- Among Latino transgender and "gender noncon-forming people," 28 percent report a household income of less than $10,000 a year, twice the rate for all transgender people and over five times the rate for all Latinos and seven times that of all Americans.[61]

How do age and generation shape the Latino community?

- Latinos make up about 18 percent of all youths in the United States ages sixteen to twenty-five. However, their share is far higher in a number of states. They make up 51 percent of all youths in New Mexico, 42 percent in California, 40 percent in Texas, 36 percent in Arizona, 31 percent in Nevada, 24 percent in Florida, and 24 percent in Colorado.[62]

- Fully two-thirds of young Latinos were born in the United States.[63]

- Interestingly, while only 21 percent of all Latinos de-scribe themselves first as "American," 50 percent of third-generation and beyond Latinos do so.[64]

- Yet only 33 percent of second-generation Latinos identify first as "American," while 41 percent identify with their country of origin.[65]

- More than two-thirds (68 percent) of young Latinos are of Mexican heritage. Growing up in families that often have less "educational capital" than other Latinos, more than four out of ten young Mexicans report that their mothers (42 percent) and fathers (44 percent) have less than a high school diploma, compared with just about one quarter of other Latinos.[66]

- The high school dropout rate for Latinos is 14 per-cent, almost three times the White high school dropout rate and twice the rate for African Americans (7 percent).[67]

◻ Latinos also have higher rates of teenage pregnancy (26 percent) than Whites (11 percent), African Americans (22 percent), and Asians (6 percent).[68]

◻ Slightly fewer Latino youth live in poverty (23 percent) than African American youth (28 percent) but more than White (13 percent) or Asian (18 percent) youth.[69]

Fully 79 percent of second-generation and 38 percent of third-generation Latinos report that they are proficient in speaking Spanish.[70]

◻ Seven in ten young Latinos say that when speaking with family members and friends, they often or sometimes use a hybrid known as *Spanglish* that mixes words from both languages.[71]

BASICS

1. Sharon R. Ennis, Merarys Ríos-Vargas, and Nora G. Albert, "The Hispanic Population: 2010," U.S. Census Bureau, May 2011, www.census.gov/prod/cen2010/briefs/c2010br-04.pdf.

2. U.S. Census Bureau, Facts for Features, "Hispanic Heritage Month 2013: Sept. 15–Oct. 15," July 2013, www.census.gov/news room/releases/archives/facts_for_features_special_editions/cb13 -ff19.html.

3. Ennis, Ríos-Vargas, and Albert, "The Hispanic Population: 2010."

4. Ibid.

5. Ibid.

6. U.S. Census Bureau, "Hispanic Heritage Month 2013: Sept. 15–Oct. 15."

7. Seth Motel and Eileen Patten, "The 10 Largest Hispanic Origin Groups: Characteristics, Rankings, Top Counties," Pew Research, Hispanic Trends Project, June 2012, www.pewhispanic .org/2012/06/27/the-10-largest-hispanic-origin-groups-characteris tics-rankings-top-counties.

8. Ennis, Ríos-Vargas, and Albert, "The Hispanic Population: 2010."

9. Ibid.

10. Mark Hugo Lopez, "5 Demographic Realities Behind the Creation of Univision/ABC News' 'Fusion' channel," Pew Research, Fact Tank, October 2013, www.pewresearch.org/fact-tank/2013/10/28/5 -demographic-realities-behind-the-creation-of-univisionabc-news -fusion-channel.

11. U.S. Census Bureau, 2012 National Population Projections: Summary Tables, www.census.gov/population/projections/data /national/2012.html.

12. Ibid.

13. U.S. Census Bureau, "Hispanic Heritage Month 2013: Sept. 15–Oct. 15."

14. Ibid.

15. Paul Taylor, Ana Gonzalez-Barrera, Jeffrey S. Passel, "An Awakened Giant: The Hispanic Electorate Is Likely to Double by 2030: Aging, Naturalization and Immigration Will Drive Growth," Pew Research, Hispanic Trends Project, November 2012, www .pewhispanic.org/2012/11/14/an-awakened-giant-the-hispanic -electorate-is-likely-to-double-by-2030.

16. Mark Hugo Lopez, Ana Gonzalez-Barrera, and Danielle Cuddington, "Diverse Origins: The Nation's 14 Largest Hispanic Origin Groups," Pew Research, Hispanic Trends Project, June 2013, www.pewhispanic.org/2013/06/19/diverse-origins-the -nations-14-largest-hispanic-origin-groups.

17. Mark Hugo Lopez, Seth Motel, and Eileen Patten, "A Record 24 Million Latinos Are Eligible to Vote, But Turnout Rate Has Lagged That of Whites, Blacks," Pew Research, Hispanic Trends

Project, October 2012, www.pewhispanic.org/2012/10/01/a-record-24 -million-latinos-are-eligible-to-vote.

18. Lopez, Gonzalez-Barrera, and Cuddington, "Diverse Origins: The Nation's 14 Largest Hispanic Origin Groups."

19. Ibid.

20. Ibid.

21. Ennis, Ríos-Vargas, and Albert, "The Hispanic Population: 2010."

22. Taylor et al., "An Awakened Giant: The Hispanic Electorate Is Likely to Double by 2030."

23. Paul Taylor, Mark Hugo Lopez, Jessica Martínez, and Gabriel Velasco, "When Labels Don't Fit: Hispanics and Their Views of Identity," Pew Research, Hispanic Trends Project, April 2012, www.pewhispanic.org/2012 /04/04/when-labels-dont-fit-hispanics-and-their-views-of-identity.

24. Ibid.

25. Pew Research, Hispanic Trends Project, "Between Two Worlds: How Young Latinos Come of Age in America," December 2009, updated July 2013, www.pewhispanic.org/2009/12/11/between-two-worlds -how-young-latinos-come-of-age-in-america.

26. Motel and Patten, "The 10 Largest Hispanic Origin Groups."

27. Taylor et al., "When Labels Don't Fit: Hispanics and Their Views of Identity."

28. Lopez, "5 Demographic Realities Behind the Creation of Univision/ ABC News' 'Fusion' Channel."

29. Taylor et al., "When Labels Don't Fit: Hispanics and Their Views of Identity."

30. Taylor et al., "An Awakened Giant: The Hispanic Electorate Is Likely to Double by 2030."

31. Motel and Patten, "The 10 Largest Hispanic Origin Groups."

32. Seth Motel and Eileen Patten, "Statistical Portrait of Hispanics in the United States, 2011," Pew Research, Hispanic Trends Project, Table 8, February 2013, www.pewhispanic.org/2013/02/15/statistical-portrait -of-hispanics-in-the-united-states-2011.

33. Computed from data provided in Taylor et al., "An Awakened Giant: The Hispanic Electorate Is Likely to Double by 2030."

34. Ennis, Ríos-Vargas, and Albert, "The Hispanic Population: 2010."

35. Taylor et al., "An Awakened Giant: The Hispanic Electorate Is Likely to Double by 2030."

36. Ibid.

37. "Latinos Set to Surpass Whites in California in March," SFGate.com, January 16, 2014, www.sfgate.com/news/article/Latinos-set-to-surpass -whites-in-California-in-5146876.php#photo-5729349.

38. Ennis, Ríos-Vargas, and Albert, "The Hispanic Population: 2010."

39. Ibid.

40. Ibid.

41. Ibid.

42. Taylor et al., "When Labels Don't Fit: Hispanics and Their Views of Identity."

IMMIGRATION

1. U.S. Census Bureau, Facts for Features, "Hispanic Heritage Month 2013: Sept. 15–Oct. 15," July 2013, www.census.gov/newsroom/releases/archives/facts_for_features_special_editions/cb13-ff19.html.

2. Mark Hugo Lopez, Ana Gonzalez-Barrera, and Danielle Cuddington, "Diverse Origins: The Nation's 14 Largest Hispanic-Origin Groups," Pew Research, Hispanic Trends Project, June 2013, www.pewhispanic.org/2013/06/19/diverse-origins-the-nations-14-largest-hispanic-origin-groups.

3. Ibid.

4. Sharon R. Ennis, Merarys Ríos-Vargas, and Nora G. Albert, "The Hispanic Population: 2010," U.S. Census Bureau, May 2011, www.census.gov/prod/cen2010/briefs/c2010br-04.pdf; Mark Hugo Lopez and Gabriel Velasco, "A Demographic Portrait of Puerto Ricans," Pew Research, Hispanic Trends Project, June 2011, www.pewhispanic.org/2011/06/13/a-demographic-portrait-of-puerto-ricans.

5. Seth Motel and Eileen Patten, Pew Research, Hispanic Trends Project, "Statistical Portrait of Hispanics in the United States, 2011," Table 10, February 2013, www.pewhispanic.org/2013/02/15/statistical-portrait-of-hispanics-in-the-united-states-2011.

6. Elizabeth M. Grieco, Yesenia D. Acosta, G. Patricia de la Cruz, Christine Gambino, Thomas Gryn, Luke J. Larsen, Edward N. Trevelyan, and Nathan P. Walters, "The Foreign-Born Population in the United States: 2010," U.S. Census Bureau, May 2012, www.census.gov/prod/2012pubs/acs-19.pdf.

7. Lopez, Gonzalez-Barrera, and Cuddington, "Diverse Origins: The Nation's 14 Largest Hispanic-Origin Groups."

8. Seth Motel and Eileen Patten, "The 10 Largest Hispanic Origin Groups: Characteristics, Rankings, Top Counties," Pew Research, Hispanic Trends Project, June 2012, www.pewhispanic.org/2012/06/27/the-10-largest-hispanic-origin-groups-characteristics-rankings-top-counties.

9. Pew Research Center, "Immigration: Key Data Points from Pew Research," March 2013, www.pewresearch.org/key-data-points/immigration-tip-sheet-on-u-s-public-opinion.

10. Ibid.

11. Pew Research, Hispanic Trends Project, "U.S. Immigrant Population Trends: A Portrait of U.S. Immigrants," February 2013, www.pewhispanic.org/2013/02/15/u-s-immigration-trends/ph_13-01-23_ss_immigration_01_title.

12. Lopez, Gonzalez-Barrera, and Cuddington, "Diverse Origins: The Nation's 14 Largest Hispanic-Origin Groups."

13. Seth Motel and Eileen Patten, Pew Research, Hispanic Trends Project, "Statistical Portrait of the Foreign-Born Population in the United States, 2011," Table 5, January 2013, www.pewhispanic.org/2013/01/29/statistical-portrait-of-the-foreign-born-population-in-the-united-states-2011; Pew Research, Hispanic Trends Project, "A Nation of Immigrants: A Portrait of the 40 Million, Including 11 Million Unauthorized," January 2013, www.pewhispanic.org/2013/01/29/a-nation-of-immigrants.

14. Motel and Patten, "The 10 Largest Hispanic Origin Groups: Characteristics, Rankings, Top Counties."

15. Lopez, Gonzalez-Barrera, and Cuddington, "Diverse Origins: The Nation's 14 Largest Hispanic Origin Groups."

16. Paul Taylor, Mark Hugo Lopez, Jessica Martínez, and Gabriel Velasco, "When Labels Don't Fit: Hispanics and Their Views of Identity," Pew Research, Hispanic Trends Project, April 2012, www.pewhispanic.org/2012/04/04/when-labels-dont-fit-hispanics-and-their-views-of-identity.

17. Ibid.

18. Ibid.

19. Ibid.

20. Ibid.

21. Lopez, Gonzalez-Barrera, and Cuddington, "Diverse Origins: The Nation's 14 Largest Hispanic Origin Groups."

22. D'vera Cohn, Ana Gonzalez-Barrera, and Danielle Cuddington, "Remittances to Latin America Recover—but Not to Mexico," Pew Research, Hispanic Trends Project, November 2013, www.pewhispanic.org/2013/11/14/3-sources-of-remittances-to-latin-america.

23. Paul Taylor, Ana Gonzalez-Barrera, Jeffrey S. Passel, and Mark Hugo Lopez, "An Awakened Giant: The Hispanic Electorate Is Likely to Double by 2030: Aging, Naturalization and Immigration Will Drive Growth," Pew Research, Hispanic Trends Project, November 2012, www.pewhispanic.org/2012/11/14/an-awakened-giant-the-hispanic-electorate-is-likely-to-double-by-2030.

24. Mark Hugo Lopez and Gabriel Velasco, "A Demographic Portrait of Puerto Ricans," Pew Research, Hispanic Trends Project, June 2011, www.pewhispanic.org/2011/06/13/a-demographic-portrait-of-puerto-ricans.

25. Ibid.

26. Mark Hugo Lopez and Ana Gonzalez-Barrera, "If They Could, How Many Unauthorized Immigrants Would Become U.S. Citizens?" Pew Research Center, June 2013, www.pewresearch.org/fact-tank/2013/06/27/if-they-could-how-many-unauthorized-immigrants-would-become-u-s-citizens.

27. Ana Gonzalez-Barrera, Mark Hugo Lopez, Jeffrey S. Passel, and Paul Taylor, "The Path Not Taken," Pew Research, Hispanic Trends Project, February 2013, www.pewhispanic.org/2013/02/04/the-path-not-taken.

28. Jeffrey S. Passel, D'vera Cohn, and Ana Gonzalez-Barrera, "Population Decline of Unauthorized Immigrants Stalls, May Have Reversed: New Estimate: 11.7 Million in 2012," Pew Research, Hispanic Trends Project, September 2013, www.pewhispanic.org/2013/09/23/population-decline-of-unauthorized-immigrants-stalls-may-have-reversed; Michael Hoefer, Nancy Rytina, and Bryan Baker, "Estimates of the Unauthorized Immigrant Population Residing in the United States: January 2011," U.S. Department of Homeland Security, www.dhs.gov/xlibrary/assets/statistics/publications/ois_ill_pe_2011.pdf.

29. Pew Research, Hispanic Trends Project, "Between Two Worlds: How Young Latinos Come of Age in America," December 2009, updated July 2013, www.pewhispanic.org/2009/12/11/between-two-worlds-how-young-latinos-come-of-age-in-america.

30. Ibid.

31. Pew Research Center, "Immigration: Key Data Points from Pew Research."

32. Passel, Cohn, and Gonzalez-Barrera, "Population Decline of Unauthorized Immigrants Stalls, May Have Reversed."

33. Francisco E. Balderrama and Raymond Rodríguez, *Decade of Betrayal: Mexican Repatriation in the 1930s* (Albuquerque: University of New Mexico Press, 1995); "Mexican Repatriation," Wikipedia, http://en.wikipedia.org/wiki/Mexican_Repatriation. Ironically, a few short years later, the U.S. initiated the Bracero Program that brought in 5 million seasonal workers from 1942 to 1964 under conditions described by the Department of Labor running the program as "legalized slavery" The Mexican Labor Program; "Braceros program," Wikipedia, http://en.wikipedia.org/wiki/Bracero_program.

34. Mark Hugo Lopez, Ana Gonzalez-Barrera, and Seth Motel, "As Deportations Rise to Record Levels, Most Latinos Oppose Obama's Policy: President's Approval Rating Drops, but He Leads 2012 Rivals," Pew Research, Hispanic Trends Project, December 2011, www.pewhispanic.org/2011/12/28/as-deportations-rise-to-record-levels-most-latinos-oppose-obamas-policy.

35. Ibid.

36. Ibid.

37. Ann Garcia, "The Facts on Immigration Today," Center for American Progress, August 14, 2013, www.americanprogress.org/wp-content/uploads/2013/04/081213_ImmigrationFastFacts-1.pdf.

38. Lopez, Gonzalez-Barrera, and Motel, "As Deportations Rise to Record Levels, Most Latinos Oppose Obama's Policy."

39. Grieco et al., "The Foreign-Born Population in the United States: 2010."

40. Ibid.

41. Ibid.

42. Ibid.

43. Roger Waldinger, "Between Here and There: How Attached Are Latinos to Their Native Country?" Pew Research, Hispanic Trends Project, October 2007, www.pewhispanic.org/2007/10/25/between-here-and-there-how-attached-are-latino-immigrants-to-their-native-country.

44. Ibid.

45. Ibid.

46. Cohn, Gonzalez-Barrera, and Cuddington, "Remittances to Latin America Recover—but Not to Mexico."

47. Pew Research, Hispanic Trends Project, "Latinos By Geography: State and County Databases: Latinos as Percent of Population By State, 2001" August 2013, www.pewhispanic.org/states.

48. Pew Research, Hispanic Trends Project, "Latinos by Geography: Demographic Profile of Hispanics in California, 2011," August 2013, www.pewhispanic.org/states/state/ca.

49. Pew Research, Hispanic Trends Project, "Latinos by Geography: Demographic Profile of Hispanics in Texas, 2011," August 2013, www.pewhispanic.org/states/state/tx.

50. Pew Research, Hispanic Trends Project, "Latinos by Geography: Demographic Profile of Hispanics in Florida, 2011," August 2013, www.pewhispanic.org/states/state/fl.

51. Pew Research, Hispanic Trends Project, "Latinos by Geography: Demographic Profile of Hispanics in New York, 2011," August 2013, www.pewhispanic.org/states/state/ny.

52. Ana Gonzalez-Barrera and Mark Hugo Lopez, "A Demographic Portrait of Mexican-Origin Hispanics in the United States," Pew Research Center, May 2013, www.pewhispanic.org/files/2013/05/2013-04_Demographic-Portrait-of-Mexicans-in-the-US.pdf.

53. Seth Motel and Eileen Patten, "Statistical Portrait of Hispanics in the United States, 2011," Pew Research, Hispanic Trends Project, February 2013, www.pewhispanic.org/2013/02/15/statistical-portrait-of-hispanics-in-the-united-states-2011.

54. Ibid.

55. Grieco, et al., "The Foreign-Born Population in the United States: 2010."

56. Ibid.

57. Motel and Patten, "Statistical Portrait of Hispanics in the United States, 2011," Table 9.

58. Mark Hugo Lopez, "5 Demographic Realities Behind the Creation of Univision/ABC News' 'Fusion' Channel," Pew Research Center, Fact Tank, October 2013, www.pewresearch.org/fact-tank/2013/10/28/5-demographic-realities-behind-the-creation-of-univisionabc-news-fusion-channel.

59. Motel and Patten, "Statistical Portrait of Hispanics in the United States, 2011," Table 9.

60. Lopez, "5 Demographic Realities Behind the Creation of Univision/ABC News' 'Fusion' Channel."

61. Grieco et al., "The Foreign-Born Population in the United States: 2010"; U.S. Census Bureau, "Average Number of People per Family Household, by Race and Hispanic Origin, Marital Status, Age, and Education of Householder: 2013," November 2013, www.census.gov/hhes/families/data/cps2013AVG.html.

62. Ibid.

63. Ibid.

64. Grieco et al., "The Foreign-Born Population in the United States: 2010."

65. Ibid.

66. Ibid.

67. Ibid.

68. Institute on Taxation and Economic Policy, "Undocumented Immigrants' State and Local Tax Contributions," July 2013, www.itep.org/pdf/undocumentedtaxes.pdf.

69. Immigration Policy Center, American Immigration Council, "Unauthorized Immigrants Pay Taxes, Too," April 2011, www.immigrationpolicy.org/sites/default/files/docs/Tax_Contributions_by_Unauthorized_Immigrants_041811.pdf.

70. National Council of La Raza, "Latinos Oppose Changes to Child

Tax Credit Fact Sheet," March 2013, www.nclr.org/images/uploads/pages /Latinos Oppose Changes to Child Tax Credit Fact Sheet 022713.pdf.

71. U.S. Department of Health and Services, "Summary of Immigrant Eligibility Restrictions Under Current Law," February 2009, http://aspe.hhs .gov/hsp/immigration/restrictions-sum.shtml.

72. Ibid.; Personal Responsibility and Work Opportunity Reconciliation Act, PL 104-193, as amended by the Illegal Immigration Reform and Immi- grant Responsibility Act, PL 104-208.

73. Centers for Medicare and Medicaid Services, Emergency Medi- cal Treatment and Labor Act (EMTALA), www.cms.gov/Regulations-and -Guidance/Legislation/EMTALA/index.html?redirect=/EMTALA.

74. National Conference of State Legislatures, Immigrant Policy Project, "State Omnibus Immigration Legislation and Legal Challenges," August 2012, www.ncsl.org/research/immigration/omnibus-immigration-legisla tion.aspx#State_Omnibus.

75. National Conference of State Legislatures, Immigrant Policy Project, "2013 Report on State Immigration Laws (Jan.–June)," September 2013, www.ncsl.org/documents/statefed/ImmigrationReport_August2013.pdf.

76. Ibid.

77. Ibid.

78. Ibid.

79. Pew Research, Center for the People and the Press, "'Borders First' a Dividing Line in Immigration Debate: More Say Legalization Would Benefit Economy than Cost Jobs," June 2013, www.people-press.org/2013/06/23 /borders-first-a-dividing-line-in-immigration-debate.

80. Pew Research Center, "Immigration: Key Data Points from Pew Research."

81. Lopez, Gonzalez-Barrera, and Motel, "As Deportations Rise to Re- cord Levels, Most Latinos Oppose Obama's Policy."

82. Mark Hugo Lopez and Ana Gonzalez-Barrera, "Latinos' Views of Il- legal Immigration's Impact on Their Community Improve," Pew Research, Hispanic Trends Project, October 2013, www.pewhispanic.org/2013/10/03 /latinos-views-of-illegal-immigrations-impact-on-their-community -improves.

83. Lopez, Gonzalez-Barrera, and Motel, "As Deportations Rise to Re- cord Levels, Most Latinos Oppose Obama's Policy."

84. Mark Hugo Lopez, Paul Taylor, Cary Funk, and Ana Gonzalez- Barrera, "On Immigration Policy, Deportation Relief Seen as More Impor- tant than Citizenship: A Survey of Hispanics and Asian Americans," Pew Research, Hispanic Trends Project, December 2013, www.pewhispanic .org/2013/12/19/on-immigration-policy-deportation-relief-seen-as-more -important-than-citizenship.

85. Pew Research Center, "Immigration: Key Data Points from Pew Research."

86. Carroll Doherty, "Attitudes Toward Immigration: In Black and White," Pew Research Center, April 2006, www.pewresearch.org/2006/04/25 /attitudes-toward-immigration-in-black-and-white.

87. Pew Research, Global Attitudes Project, "World Publics Wel- come Global Trade—but Not Immigration: 47-Nation Pew Global

Attitudes Survey," October 2007, www.pewglobal.org/2007/10/04/world
-publics-welcome-global-trade-but-not-immigration.

88. Mark Hugo Lopez and Ana Gonzalez-Barrera, "Latino Voters Support Obama by 3-1 Ratio, but Are Less Certain than Others About Voting," Pew Research, Hispanic Trends Project, October 2012, www.pewhispanic.org/2012/10/11/latino-voters-support-obama-by-3-1-ratio-but-are-less-certain-than-others-about-voting.

89. Ibid.

90. Immigration Policy Center, American Immigration Council, "Who and Where the DREAMers Are," August 2012, www.immigrationpolicy.org/just-facts/who-and-where-dreamers-are.

91. Congressional Budget Office, S. 744—Border Security, Economic Opportunity, and Immigration Modernization Act, 2013, www.cbo.gov/publication/44397, cited in "The Facts on Immigration Today," Center for American Progress, August 2013, www.americanprogress.org/wp-content/uploads/2013/04/081213_ImmigrationFastFacts-1.pdf.

92. Ibid.

VOTING AND POLITICS

1. Mark Hugo Lopez, Seth Motel, and Eileen Patten, "A Record 24 Million Latinos Are Eligible to Vote, but Turnout Rate Has Lagged That of Whites, Blacks," Pew Research, Hispanic Trends Project, October 2012, www.pewhispanic.org/2012/10/01/a-record-24-million-latinos-are-eligible-to-vote.

2. Ibid.

3. Paul Taylor, Ana Gonzalez-Barrera, Jeffrey S. Passel, and Mark Hugo Lopez, "An Awakened Giant: The Hispanic Electorate Is Likely to Double by 2030: Aging, Naturalization and Immigration Will Drive Growth," Pew Research, Hispanic Trends Project, November 2012, www.pewhispanic.org/2012/11/14/an-awakened-giant-the-hispanic-electorate-is-likely-to-double-by-2030.

4. Ibid.

5. Ibid.

6. Ibid.

7. Ibid.

8. U.S. Census Bureau, "The Diversifying Electorate—Voting Rates by Race and Hispanic Origin in 2012 (and Other Recent Elections)," Current Population Survey, May 2013, www.census.gov/prod/2013pubs/p20-568.pdf.

9. Mark Hugo Lopez and Ana Gonzalez-Barrera, "Inside the 2012 Latino Electorate," Pew Research, Hispanic Trends Project, June 2013, www.pewhispanic.org/2013/06/03/inside-the-2012-latino-electorate.

10. Gabriel R. Sanchez, "The Untapped Potential of the Latino Electorate," Latino Decisions, January 2013, www.latinodecisions.com/blog/2013/01/15/the-untapped-potential-of-the-latino-electorate.

11. Lopez and Gonzalez-Barrera, "Inside the 2012 Latino Electorate."

12. Ibid.

13. Ibid.

14. Ibid.

15. Ibid.

16. Ibid.

17. Ibid.

18. Ibid.

19. Mark Hugo Lopez and Paul Taylor, Pew Research, Hispanic Trends Project, "Latino Voters in the 2012 Elections," November 2012, www .pewhispanic.org/2012/11/07/latino-voters-in-the-2012-election.

20. Ibid.

21. Ibid.

22. Ibid.

23. Ibid.

24. Ibid.

25. Pew Research, Religion and Public Life Project, "Latinos, Religion and Campaign 2012," October 2012, www.pewforum.org/2012/10/18 /latinos-religion-and-campaign-2012.

26. Ibid.

27. Ibid.

28. Ibid.

29. Ibid.

30. Democratic National Committee, Our Party, Our Leaders, 2014, www.democrats.org/about/our_leaders.

31. Sandra Lilley, "Over 800 Latino Delegates Ready to Rally for Obama as Democratic Convention Begins Today," NBC Latino, September 2012, http://nbclatino.com/2012/09/04/over-800-latino-democrats-ready-to -rally-for-obama-as-convention-begins-today.

32. Luis R. Fraga, John A. Garcia, Rodney E. Hero, Michael Jones-Correa, Valerie Martinez-Ebers, and Gary M. Segura, Latinos in the New Millennium (New York: Cambridge University Press, 2012).

33. Wendy R. Weiser and Lawrence Norden, "Voting Law Changes in 2012," Brennan Center for Justice at New York University School of Law, October 2011, www.brennancenter.org/sites/default/files/legacy/Democ racy/VRE/Brennan_Voting_Law_V10.pdf.

34. Brennan Center for Justice at New York University School of Law, "Voting Laws Roundup 2013," December 2013, www.brennancenter.org /analysis/election-2013-voting-laws-roundup.

35. Keith Bentele and Erin O'Brien, "States with Higher Black Turnout Are More Likely to Restrict Voting," Washington Post, December 2013, www.washingtonpost.com/blogs/monkey-cage/wp/2013/12/17/states -with-higher-black-turnout-are-more-likely-to-restrict-voting/?clsrd.

36. Mark Hugo Lopez and Ana Gonzalez-Barrera, "Latino Voters Support Obama by 3-1 Ratio, but Are Less Certain than Others About Voting," Pew Research, Hispanic Trends Project, October 2012, www.pewhis panic.org/2012/10/11/latino-voters-support-obama-by-3-1-ratio-but-are -less-certain-than-others-about-voting; Weiser and Norden, "Voting Law Changes in 2012,."

37. The Sentencing Project, Felony Disenfranchisement, 2013, www .sentencingproject.org/template/page.cfm?id=133.

38. Paul Taylor, Mark Hugo Lopez, Jessica Martínez, and Gabriel Velasco, "When Labels Don't Fit: Hispanics and Their Views of Identity," Pew

Research, Hispanic Trends Project, April 2012, www.pewhispanic.org/2012/04/04/when-labels-dont-fit-hispanics-and-their-views-of-identity.

39. Ibid.

40. Ibid.

41. Lopez and Gonzalez-Barrera, "Latino Voters Support Obama by 3-1 Ratio, but Are Less Certain than Others About Voting."

42. Mark Hugo Lopez, Ana Gonzalez-Barrera, and Seth Motel, "As Deportations Rise to Record Levels, Most Latinos Oppose Obama's Policy: President's Approval Rating Drops, but He Leads 2012 Rivals," Pew Research, Hispanic Trends Project, December 2011, www.pewhispanic.org/2011/12/28/as-deportations-rise-to-record-levels-most-latinos-oppose-obamas-policy.

43. Taylor et al., "When Labels Don't Fit: Hispanics and Their Views of Identity."

44. Ibid.

45. Lopez, Gonzalez-Barrera, and Motel, "As Deportations Rise to Record Levels, Most Latinos Oppose Obama's Policy."

46. Wendy Wang, "The Rise of Intermarriage: Rates, Characteristics Vary by Race and Gender," Pew Research, Social and Demographic Trends, February 2012, www.pewsocialtrends.org/2012/02/16/the-rise-of-intermarriage.

47. Adrian Pantoja, "Latinos Remain Committed to Reducing Air Pollution and Preventing Climate Change," Latino Decisions, May 2013, www.latinodecisions.com/blog/2013/05/07/latinos-remain-committed-to-reducing-air-pollution-and-preventing-climate-change; Sierra Club and National Council of La Raza, "2012 National Latinos and the Environment Survey," http://vault.sierraclub.org/ecocentro/survey/2012%20Latinos%20and%20the%20Environment%20Survey_Exec%20Summary_English.pdf

48. Office of the Clerk, U.S. House of Representatives, Congressional Profile, 2013, http://clerk.house.gov/member_info/cong.aspx.

49. Huffington Post, "Latino Congress Members: 2012 Election Sets a New Record with the Most Latinos Elected to U.S. Senate, House in History," November 2012, www.huffingtonpost.com/2012/11/07/latino-congress-members_n_2090311.html.

50. Ibid.

51. Ibid.

52. Answers.USA.gov, "Presidential Cabinet," December 2013, http://answers.usa.gov/system/templates/selfservice/USAGov/#!portal/1012/article/4434/Presidential-Cabinet.

53. Lisa Lerer, "Obama Diversity Promise Makes Second Cabinet Like First," Bloomberg Politics, April 2013, http://www.bloomberg.com/news/2013-04-30/obama-diversity-promise-makes-second-cabinet-like-first.html.

54. The "Plum Book" is a directory of presidential political appointees in the federal government; Hispanic Career World, "Perez as U.S. Secretary of Labor Welcomed by National Latino Leaders," Equal Opportunity Publications, Summer/Fall 2013, www.eop.com/hcw_article.php?content=PerezAsUSSecretaryOfLaborWelcomedByNationalLatinoLeaders.

55. The White House, White House Profiles, January 2014, www.white house.gov/blog/authors.

56. Supreme Court of the United States, FAQ—Justices, last updated January 2014, www.supremecourt.gov/faq_justices.aspx#faqjustice16.

57. Federal Judicial Center, Diversity on the Bench: Hispanic Judges on the Federal Courts, 2013, www.fjc.gov/servlet/nDsearch?race=Hispanic.

58. Data extrapolated from Federal Judicial Center, Biographical Directory of Federal Judges (by Hispanic Origin and electing president: Barack Obama, George W. Bush, William Clinton), 2013, www.fjc.gov/public/home.nsf/hisj.

59. American Judicature Society, Diversity of the Bench, 2011, www.judicialselection.com/judicial_selection/bench_diversity/index.cfm?state=.

60. NALEO Education Fund, 2011 Directory of Latino Elected Officials, 2011, www.naleo.org/directory.html.

61. Ibid.

62. Ibid.

63. Rutgers Center on the American Governor, Fast Facts About American Governors, 2013, http://governors.rutgers.edu/on-governors/us-governors/fast-facts-about-american-governors.

64. National Hispanic Caucus of State Legislators, Hispanic State Legislators at a Glance, 2014, www.nhcsl.org/hispanic-state-legislator-information.php.

65. Ibid.

66. Adriana Maestas, "Underrepresented in City Hall: a Look at U.S. Latino Mayors," NBC Latino, November 2013, http://nbclatino.com/2013/11/02/underrepresented-in-city-hall-a-look-at-the-latino-mayors-in-the-united-states.

67. Ted Sherman/Star-Ledger, "Luis Quintana Sworn in as Newark's First Latino Mayor, Filling Unexpired Term of Cory Booker," NJ.com, November 2013, www.nj.com/essex/index.ssf/2013/11/luis_quintana_sworn_in_as_newarks_first_latino_mayor_filling_unexpired_term_of_cory_booker.html; Susana G. Baumann, "Latino Mayors, Revitalize Cities and Push Towards Economic Growth," Voxxi, October 2013, http://voxxi.com/2013/10/15/latino-mayors-revitalizing-cities/#ixzz2huyQrZ70; Tom Dotan, "Latino Texas: 'San Antonio Is a Peek at the America of Tomorrow': Mayor Julián Castro's Democratic Vision for the Future Is Clear, but It Is Built on a Difficult Past and a Frustrating Present," The Guardian, October 2012, http://www.theguardian.com/world/2012/oct/06/san-antonio-texas-elections-democrats-republicans; Sandra Lilley, "Latino Mayors in the Trenches on Gun Control, Immigration," NBC Latino, January 2013, http://nbclatino.com/2013/01/17/latino-mayors-in-the-trenches-on-gun-control-immigration; Bill Hart and E.C. Hedberg, "Arizona's Emerging Latino Vote," Morrison Institute for Public Policy at Arizona State University, 2012, http://sod208.fulton.asu.edu/publications-reports/2012-arizonas-emerging-latino-vote.

68. Mark Hugo Lopez, Pew Research, Hispanic Trends Project, "Three-Fourths of Hispanics Say Their Community Needs a Leader: Most Latinos Cannot Name One," October 2013, www.pewhispanic.org/2013/10/22/three-fourths-of-hispanics-say-their-community-needs-a-leader.

69. Ibid.

70. Ibid.

JOBS AND THE ECONOMY

1. U.S. Congress Joint Economic Committee, "America's Hispanic Population: An Economic Snapshot," October 2013, www.jec.senate.gov/public/?a=Files.Serve&File_id=7a08df2f-2485-422d-806e-0c239 bebab5a.

2. Ibid.

3. Ibid.

4. U.S. Department of Labor, "The Latino Labor Force in the Recovery," April 2012, www.dol.gov/_sec/media/reports/hispaniclaborforce.

5. U.S. Census Bureau, Facts for Features, "Hispanic Heritage Month 2013: Sept. 15–Oct. 15," July 2013, www.census.gov/newsroom/releases/archives/facts_for_features_special_editions/cb13-ff19.html.

6. Diana Furchtgott-Roth, "The Economic Benefits of Immigration," Manhattan Institute for Policy Research, February 2013, www.manhattan-institute.org/html/ib_18.htm#.UokoFZRgaOc.

7. Bureau of Labor Statistics, "The Employment Situation—December 2013," USDL-14-0002, January 2014, www.bls.gov/news.release/archives/empsit_01102014.htm.

8. U.S. Congress Joint Economic Committee, "America's Hispanic Population: An Economic Snapshot."

9. Bureau of Labor Statistics, Employment Situation Summary: Table A-3. Employment status of the Hispanic or Latino population by sex and age, December 2013, www.bls.gov/news.release/empsit.t03.htm.

10. U.S. Congress Joint Economic Committee, "America's Hispanic Population: An Economic Snapshot."

11. Ibid.

12. Ibid.

13. U.S. Department of Labor, "The Latino Labor Force at a Glance," April 2012, www.dol.gov/_sec/media/reports/HispanicLaborForce/Hispanic LaborForce.pdf.

14. Algernon Austin, "Unemployment Rates Are Projected to Remain High for Whites, Latinos, and African Americans Throughout 2013," Economic Policy Institute, February 2013, www.epi.org/publication/unemployment-rates-whites-latinos-african-americans.

15. U.S. Congress Joint Economic Committee, "America's Hispanic Population: An Economic Snapshot."

16. AFL-CIO, "The Elusive American Dream: Lower Wages, High Unemployment and an Uncertain Retirement for Latinos," August 2013, www.aflcio.org/content/download/98601/2662151/file/LatinoReport.pdf.

17. Hector E. Sanchez, Andrea L. Delgado, Diana Villa, Ian Paul Fetterolf, and Juan Sebastian Velasquez, "Trabajadoras: Challenges and Conditions of Latina Workers in the United States," Labor Council for Latin American Advancement (LCLAA), March 2012, www.lclaa.org/images/pdf/Trabajadoras_Report.pdf.

18. Rakesh Kochhar, "The Demographics of the Jobs Recovery: Employment Gains by Race, Ethnicity, Gender and Nativity," Pew Research,

Hispanic Trends Project, March 2012, www.pewhispanic.org/2012/03/21/the-demographics-of-the-jobs-recovery.

19. U.S. Congress Joint Economic Committee, "America's Hispanic Population: An Economic Snapshot."

20. Ibid.

21. U.S. Department of Labor, "The Latino Labor Force at a Glance."

22. Sanchez et al., "Trabajadoras: Challenges and Conditions of Latina Workers in the United States."

23. U.S. Department of Agriculture, Economic Research Service, "Farm Labor," www.ers.usda.gov/topics/farm-economy/farm-labor/background#demographic.

24. Centers for Disease Control and Prevention, "CDC Health Disparities and Inequalities Report—United States, 2013," November 2013, www.cdc.gov/mmwr/pdf/other/su6203.pdf.

25. U.S. Census Bureau, "Hispanic Heritage Month 2013: Sept. 15–Oct. 15."

26. Geoscape and U.S. Hispanic Chamber of Commerce, "Hispanic Businesses and Entrepreneurs Drive Growth in the New Economy," 2013, www.geoscape.com/hbr/pdf/Geoscape_HispanicBusinessOwners_FINAL.pdf.

27. Ibid.

28. U.S. Department of Labor, "The Latino Labor Force at a Glance."

29. Ibid.

30. U.S. Office of Personnel Management, "Twelfth Annual Report to the President on Hispanic Employment in the Federal Government," September 2013, www.opm.gov/policy-data-oversight/diversity-and-inclusion/reports/hispanic_sep2013.pdf.

31. Ibid.

32. D5 Coalition, "State of the Work, 2013: Inspiration and Ideas for Advancing Diversity, Equity, and Inclusion in Philanthropy," 2013, www.d5coalition.org/wp-content/uploads/2013/05/D5_State_of_the_Work_2013.pdf.

33. U.S. Department of Defense, "2012 Demographics: Profile of the Military Community," 2012, www.militaryonesource.mil/12038/MOS/Reports/2012_Demographics_Report.pdf.

34. U.S. Air Force, Air Force Personnel Demographics, www.afpc.af.mil/library/airforcepersonneldemographics.asp.

35. U.S. Navy, "Navy Honors Service, Leadership During 2013 Hispanic American Heritage Month," September 2012, www.navy.mil/submit/display.asp?story_id=76526.

36. U.S. Marine Corps, "The Marine Corps, 'A Young and Vigorous Force': Demographics Update," June 2013, www.manpower.usmc.mil/portal/page/portal/MRA_HOME2/Related%20Links/Demographics%20Booklet%20June%202013.pdf

37. U.S. Department of Defense, "The Demographic Composition of Today's Military Leadership," in "From Representation to Inclusion: Diversity Leadership for the 21st-Century Military," 2011, http://diversity.defense.gov/Portals/51/Documents/Special%20Feature/MLDC_Final_Report.pdf.

38. U.S. Census Bureau, "Hispanic Heritage Month 2013: Sept. 15–Oct. 15."

39. National Center for Veterans Analysis and Statistics, "Minority Veterans: 2011," May 2013, www.va.gov/vetdata/docs/SpecialReports/Minority_Veterans_2011.pdf.

40. Ibid.

41. Bureau of Labor Statistics, "Employment Situation of Veterans—2012," March 2013, http://www.bls.gov/news.release/archives/vet_0320 2013.pdf.

42. Ibid.

43. National Center for Veterans Analysis and Statistics, "Minority Veterans: 2011," May 2013, http://www.va.gov/vetdata/docs/SpecialReports /Minority_Veterans_2011.pdf.

44. Center of Military History, U.S. Army, "Hispanic American Medal of Honor Recipients," last updated 2011, http://www.history.army.mil/html /topics/hispam/hisp-moh.html

45. Pew Research, Hispanic Trends Project, "Hispanic Population Trends," February 2013, www.pewhispanic.org/2013/02/15/hispanic-popu lation-trends/ph_13-01-23_ss_hispanics13.

46. Ibid.

47. Vanessa Cárdenas, "10 Facts About Latino Women and Pay Inequity," Center for American Progress, April 2012, www.american progress.org/issues/women/news/2012/04/16/11365/10-facts-about -latino-women-and-pay-inequity.

48. AFL-CIO, "The Elusive American Dream: Lower Wages, High Unemployment and an Uncertain Retirement for Latinos."

49. U.S. Congress Joint Economic Committee, "America's Hispanic Population: An Economic Snapshot."

50. U.S. Bureau of Labor Statistics, "Highlights of Women's Earnings in 2012," Report 1045, October 2013, www.bls.gov/cps/cpswom2012.pdf.

51. AFL-CIO, "The Elusive American Dream: Lower Wages, High Unemployment and an Uncertain Retirement for Latinos."

52. Nielsen Company, "State of the Hispanic Consumer: The Hispanic Market Imperative," 2012, www.nielsen.com/content/dam/corporate/us /en/reports-downloads/2012-Reports/State-of-the-Hispanic-Consumer .pdf.a

53. U.S. Census Bureau, "Hispanic Heritage Month 2013: Sept. 15–Oct. 15."

54. Ana Gonzalez-Barrera and Mark Hugo Lopez, "A Demographic Portrait of Mexican-Origin Hispanics in the United States," Pew Research Center, Pew Hispanic Center, May 2013, www.pewhispanic.org /files/2013/05/2013-04_Demographic-Portrait-of-Mexicans-in-the-US.pdf.

55. AFL-CIO, "The Elusive American Dream: Lower Wages, High Unemployment and an Uncertain Retirement for Latinos."

56. Elizabeth M. Grieco, Yesenia D. Acosta, G. Patricia de la Cruz, Christine Gambino, Thomas Gryn, Luke J. Larsen, Edward N. Trevelyan, and Nathan P. Walters, "The Foreign-Born Population in the United States: 2010," U.S. Census Bureau, May 2012, www.census.gov/prod/2012pubs/acs-19 .pdf.

57. Ibid.

58. Centers for Disease Control and Prevention, "CDC Health Disparities and Inequalities Report—United States, 2013."

59. U.S. Department of Labor, "The Latino Labor Force at a Glance."

60. Sanchez et al., "Trabajadoras: Challenges and Conditions of Latina Workers in the United States."

61. Centers for Disease Control and Prevention, "CDC Health Disparities and Inequalities Report—United States, 2013."

62. Sanchez et al., "Trabajadoras: Challenges and Conditions of Latina Workers in the United States."

63. Race/ethnicity was not indicated in 37 percent of documented injuries. Bureau of Labor Statistics, "Nonfatal Occupational Injuries and Illnesses Requiring Days Away from Work, 2012," Report USDL-13-2257, November 2013, www.bls.gov/news.release/pdf/osh2.pdf.

64. CareerBuilder, "2011 Diversity in the Workplace: A CareerBuilder Study," June 2011, http://img.icbdr.com/images/jp/pdf/BRO-0053_DiversityReport_2011.pdf.

65. Hector E. Sanchez, Andrea L. Delgado, and Rosa G. Saavedra, "Latino Workers in the United States, 2011" Labor Council for Latin American Advancement (LCLAA), April 2011, www.lclaa.org/images/pdf/LCLAA_Report.pdf.

66. Ibid.

67. Sanchez et al., Trabajadoras: Challenges and Conditions of Latina Workers in the United States."

68. Ibid.

69. Ibid.

70. Jaime M. Grant, Lisa A. Mottet, and Justin Tanis, "Injustice at Every Turn: A Report of the National Transgender Discrimination Survey," National Gay and Lesbian Task Force and National Center for Transgender Equality, February 2011, www.thetaskforce.org/downloads/reports/reports/ntds_full.pdf.

71. Bureau of Labor Statistics, "Union Members–2012," January 2013, www.bls.gov/news.release/archives/union2_01232013.htm.

72. Ibid.

73. Ibid.

74. Geoscape and U.S. Hispanic Chamber of Commerce, "Hispanic Businesses and Entrepreneurs Drive Growth in the New Economy."

75. Alexandra Bjerg, "Hispanic-Owned Businesses Fueling the Economic Recovery in California," California Economic Summit, October 2013, www.caeconomy.org/reporting/entry/hispanic-owned-businesses-fueling-the-economic-recovery-in-california.

76. Geoscape and U.S. Hispanic Chambers of Commerce, "Hispanic Businesses and Entrepreneurs Drive Growth in the New Economy."

77. Ibid.

78. Bjerg, "Hispanic-owned Businesses Fueling the Economic Recovery in California."

79. Geoscape and U.S. Hispanic Chamber of Commerce, "Hispanic Businesses and Entrepreneurs Drive Growth in the New Economy."

80. D'Vera Cohn, Ana Gonzalez-Barrera and Danielle, "Remittances to

Latin America Recover—but Not to Mexico," Pew Research Center, Hispanic Trends Project, November 2013, www.pewhispanic.org/2013/11/15/remittances-to-latin-america-recover-but-not-to-mexico.

81. Ibid.

82. Arloc Sherman, Robert Greenstein, and Kathy Ruffing, "'Contrary to 'Entitlement Society' Rhetoric, over Nine-Tenths of Entitlement Benefits Go to Elderly, Disabled, or Working Households," Center on Budget and Policy Priorities, February 2012, hwww.cbpp.org/files/2-10-12pov.pdf.

83. Pew Research, Hispanic Trends Project, "Hispanic Population Trends."

84. Social Security Administration, "Social Security Is Important to Hispanics," February 2013, www.ssa.gov/pressoffice/factsheets/hispanics-alt.pdf.

85. Rich Morin, "The Politics and Demographics of Food Stamp Recipients," Pew Research Center, July 2013, www.pewresearch.org/fact-tank/2013/07/12/the-politics-and-demographics-of-food-stamp-recipients.

86. Mareshah Jackson, "Fact Sheet: The State of Latinas in the United States," Center for American Progress, November 2013, www.americanprogress.org/issues/race/report/2013/11/07/79167/fact-sheet-the-state-of-latinas-in-the-united-states.

87. U.S. Congress Joint Economic Committee, "America's Hispanic Population: An Economic Snapshot."

88. Institute on Taxation and Economic Policy, "Undocumented Immigrants' State and Local Tax Contributions," July 2013, www.itep.org/pdf/undocumentedtaxes.pdf.

89. U.S. Government Printing Office, "Economic Report of the President, Transmitted to the Congress February 2005," www.presidency.ucsb.edu/economic_reports/2005.pdf; Immigration Policy Center, American Immigration Council, "Unauthorized Immigrants Pay Taxes, Too," April 2011, www.immigrationpolicy.org/sites/default/files/docs/Tax_Contributions_by_Unauthorized_Immigrants_041811.pdf.

90. Signe-Mary McKernan, Caroline Ratcliffe, Eugene Steuerle, and Sisi Zhang, "Less than Equal: Racial Disparities in Wealth Accumulation," Urban Institute, April 2013, www.urban.org/UploadedPDF/412802-Less-Than-Equal-Racial-Disparities-in-Wealth-Accumulation.pdf.

91. Pew Research Center, Social and Demographic Trends Project, "King's Dream Remains an Elusive Goal; Many Americans See Racial Disparities," August 2013, www.pewsocialtrends.org/files/2013/08/final_full_report_racial_disparities.pdf.

92. McKernan, et al., "Less than Equal: Racial Disparities in Wealth Accumulation," Urban Institute, April 2013, www.urban.org/UploadedPDF/412802-Less-Than-Equal-Racial-Disparities-in-Wealth-Accumulation.pdf.

93. Rakesh Kochhar, Richard Fry, and Paul Taylor, "Wealth Gaps Rise to Record Highs Between Whites, Blacks, Hispanics: Twenty-to-One," Pew Research Center, Social and Demographic Trends Project, July 2011, www.pewsocialtrends.org/2011/07/26/wealth-gaps-rise-to-record-highs-between-whites-blacks-hispanics.

94. Ibid.

95. Ibid.

96. Pew Research, Hispanic Trends Project, "Hispanic Population Trends."

97. Alejandro Becerra, "State of Hispanic Homeownership Report," National Association of Hispanic Real Estate Professionals, 2012, http://nahrep.org/downloads/state-of-homeownership.pdf.

98. Gonzalez-Barrera and Lopez, "A Demographic Portrait of Mexican-Origin Hispanics in the United States."

99. Christian E. Weller, Julie Ajinkya, and Jane Farrell, "The State of Communities of Color in the U.S. Economy: Still Feeling the Pain Three Years into the Recovery." Center for American Progress, April 2012, www.americanprogress.org/wp-content/uploads/issues/2012/04/pdf/comm_of_color.pdf.

100. Becerra, "State of Hispanic Homeownership Report."

101. Census Transportation Planning Products, "Vehicle Availability and Mode to Work by Race and Hispanic Origin, 2011," U.S. Department of Transportation, Federal Highway Administration, www.fhwa.dot.gov/planning/census_issues/ctpp/articles/vamtw.cfm.

102. National Automobile Dealers Association, "Dealers Reveal Secrets to Win the Hispanic Market," 2013, www.nadaconvention.org/nada2013/Custom/Handout/Speaker0_Session1545_1.pdf.

103. Ibid.

104. Federal Deposit Insurance Corporation, "2011 FDIC National Survey of Unbanked and Underbanked Households," September 2012, www.fdic.gov/householdsurvey/2012_unbankedreport.pdf.

105. Ibid.

106. Nari Rhee, "Race and Retirement Insecurity in the United States," National Institute on Retirement Security, December 2013, www.nirsonline.org/storage/nirs/documents/Race%20and%20Retirement%20Insecurity/race_and_retirement_insecurity_final.pdf.

107. Ibid.

108. Ibid.

109. Ibid.

110. Ibid.

111. Federal Deposit Insurance Corporation, "2011 FDIC National Survey of Unbanked and Underbanked Households."

112. Ibid.

113. Nielsen Company, "Latina Power Shift," 2013, www.nielsen.com/content/dam/corporate/us/en/reports-downloads/2013%20Reports/Nielsen-Latina-Report-2013.pdf.

114. Ibid.

115. Mark Hugo Lopez, "U.S. Hispanics and the Nation's Economy," Pew Research Center, Hispanic Trends Project, presented at the Border Economic Development and Entrepreneurship Symposium, November 2013, www.dallasfed.org/assets/documents/research/events/2013/13bedes_lopez.pdf.

116. Nielsen Company, "Upscale Latinos: America's New Baby Boomers," June 2013, www.nielsen.com/us/en/newswire/2013/upscale-latinos--americas-new-baby-boomers.html.

117. Amy Traub and Catherine Ruetschlin, "The Plastic Safety Net: Findings from the 2012 National Survey on Credit Card Debt of Low- and Middle-Income Households," Dēmos, May 2012, www.demos.org/sites/default/files/publications/PlasticSafetyNet-Demos.pdf.

118. Catherine Ruetschlin and Dedrick Asante-Muhammad, "The Challenge of Credit Card Debt for the African American Middle Class," Dēmos and NAACP, December 2013, www.demos.org/sites/default/files/publications/CreditCardDebt-Demos_NAACP_0.pdf.

119. Ibid.

120. PNC Financial Services Group, Inc., "20-Somethings Hispanic Are More Optimistic," September 2013, www.pnc.com/webapp/unsec/Requester?resource=/wps/wcm/connect/af47a5004111e4209140dd4767a73868/PNCFinancialIndependence_Hispanic_9513.pdf?MOD=AJPERES&CACHEID=af47a5004111e4209140dd4767a73868.

121. Traub and Ruetschlin, "The Plastic Safety Net."

122. Hispanic Association on Corporate Responsibility, "Corporate Governance Study," 2013, www.hacr.org/images/2013_HACR_Corporate_Governance_Study_CGS.pdf.

123. Ibid.

124. Ibid.

125. Ibid.

126. Ibid.

127. American Bar Association, Commission on Hispanic Legal Rights and Responsibilities, "Latinos in the United States: Overcoming Legal Obstacles, Engaging in Civic Life," 2013, www.americanbar.org/content/dam/aba/images/commission_on_hispanic_legal_rights_responsibilities/hispanicreportnew.pdf.

128. Bureau of Labor Statistics, "Volunteering in the United States—2012," February 2013, www.bls.gov/news.release/volun.nr0.htm.

129. Geoscape and U.S. Hispanic Chambers of Commerce, "Hispanic Businesses and Entrepreneurs Drive Growth in the New Economy."

130. Ibid.

131. Nielsen Company, "Latina Power Shift."

132. Nielsen Company, "State of the Hispanic Consumer: The Hispanic Market Imperative."

133. Nielsen Company, "Latina Power Shift."

134. Associated Press, "Salsa Outsells Ketchup as American Tastes Change," retrieved from Fox News, October 2013, www.foxnews.com/leisure/2013/10/17/changing-face-america-is-influencing-our-taste-buds-one-tortilla-chip-at-time.

135. Nielsen Company, "State of the Hispanic Consumer: The Hispanic Market Imperative."

136. Association of Hispanic Advertising Agencies (AHAA), "Hispanic Fast Facts," last updated September 2013, www.ahaa.org/default.asp?contentID=161.

137. Nielsen Company, "Latina Power Shift."

138. "Hispanic Fact Pack 2013: Advertising Age's Annual Guide to Hispanic Marketing and Media," Ad Age Data Center, July 2013, http://adage.com/trend-reports/report.php?id=78; Michael Sebastian, "First-Quarter

Ad Spending Comes in Flat: Broadcast TV Declines Partly Because of Prime-Time Ratings Erosion," *Advertising Age*, June 2013, http://adage .com/article/media/ad-spending-flat-quarter/242829.

139. Nielsen Company, "State of the Hispanic Consumer: The Hispanic Market Imperative."

140. Ibid.

FAMILY AND COMMUNITY

1. U.S. Census Bureau, Facts for Features, "Hispanic Heritage Month 2013: Sept. 15–Oct. 15," July 2013, www.census.gov/newsroom/releases /archives/facts_for_features_special_editions/cb13-ff19.html.

2. Daphne Lofquist, Terry Lugaila, Martin O'Connell, and Sarah Feliz, "Households and Families: 2010," U.S. Census Bureau, April 2012, www .census.gov/prod/cen2010/briefs/c2010br-14.pdf.

3. U.S. Census Bureau, "Average Number of People per Family Household, by Race And Hispanic Origin, Marital Status, Age, and Education of Householder: 2013," November 2013, www.census.gov/hhes/families /data/cps2013AVG.html.

4. Elizabeth M. Grieco, Yesenia D. Acosta, G. Patricia de la Cruz, Christine Gambino, Thomas Gryn, Luke J. Larsen, Edward N. Trevelyan, and Nathan P. Walters, "The Foreign-Born Population in the United States: 2010," U.S. Census Bureau, May 2012, www.census.gov/prod/2012pubs/acs-19 .pdf.

5. Jonathan Vespa, Jamie M. Lewis, and Rose M. Kreider, "America's Families and Living Arrangements: 2012," U.S. Census Bureau, August 2013, www.census.gov/prod/2013pubs/p20-570.pdf.

6. "A Nation of Immigrants: A Portrait of the 40 Million, Including 11 Million Unauthorized," Pew Research, Hispanic Trends Project, January 2013, www.pewhispanic.org/2013/01/29/a-nation-of-immigrants; Jeffrey S. Passel and Paul Taylor, "Unauthorized Immigrants and Their U.S.-Born Children," Pew Research Center, Pew Hispanic Center, August 2010, www .pewhispanic.org/files/reports/125.pdf.

7. Vespa, Lewis, and Kreider, "America's Families and Living Arrangements: 2012."

8. Vespa, Lewis, and Kreider, "America's Families and Living Arrangements: 2012."

9. Seth Motel and Eileen Patten, "Statistical Portrait of Hispanics in the United States, 2011," Pew Research, Hispanic Trends Project, Table 19, February 2013, www.pewhispanic.org/2013/02/15/statistical -portrait-of-hispanics-in-the-united-states-2011.

10. Federal Interagency Forum on Child and Family Statistics, "America's Children: Key National Indicators of Well-Being, 2013," 2013, www .childstats.gov/pdf/ac2013/ac_13.pdf.

11. ChildStats.gov, Table FAM1.A: Family Structure and Children's Living Arrangements: Percentage of Children Ages 0–17 by Presence of Parents in Household and Race and Hispanic Origin, 1980–2012, 2013, www.childstats.gov/americaschildren/tables/fam1a.asp?popup=true.

12. Federal Interagency Forum on Child and Family Statistics, "America's Children: Key National Indicators of Well-Being, 2013."

13. Data is on activity limitation: "Activity limitation refers to a person's inability, due to a chronic physical, mental, emotional, or behavioral condition, to participate fully in age-appropriate activities." Federal Interagency Forum on Child and Family Statistics, "America's Children: Key National Indicators of Well-Being, 2013."

14. Erica Saylor, "Hispanic Millennials: Living at Home, Delaying Marriage, and Focusing on College," Blog.Viacom, January 2014, http://blog.viacom.com/2014/01/hispanic-millennials-living-at-home-delaying-marriage-and-focusing-on-college/#sthash.AaLiEjOF.30TeKbMQ.dpuf.

15. Casey E. Copen, Kimberly Daniels, Jonathan Vespa, and William D. Mosher, "National Health Statistics Reports: First Marriages in the United States: Data from the 2006–2010 National Survey of Family Growth," U.S. Department of Health and Human Services, March 2012, www.cdc.gov/nchs/data/nhsr/nhsr049.pdf.

16. Ibid.

17. U.S. Census Bureau, American Fact Finder, Table S1201: Marital Status: 2012 American Community Survey 1-Year Estimates, http://factfinder2.census.gov/faces/tableservices/jsf/pages/productview.xhtml?pid=ACS_12_1YR_S1201&prodType=table.

18. Ibid.

19. U.S. Census Bureau, Facts for Features, "Hispanic Heritage Month 2013: Sept. 15–Oct. 15."

20. U.S. Census Bureau, Table FG1: Married Couple Family Groups, by Labor Force Status of Both Spouses, and Race and Hispanic Origin/1 of the Reference Person: 2010, www.census.gov/population/www/socdemo/hh-fam/cps2010.html.

21. Wendy Wang, "The Rise of Intermarriage: Rates, Characteristics Vary by Race and Gender," Pew Research, Social and Demographic Trends, February 2012, www.pewsocialtrends.org/2012/02/16/the-rise-of-intermarriage.

22. Ibid.

23. Ibid.

24. Ibid.

25. "Between Two Worlds: How Young Latinos Come of Age in America," Pew Research, Hispanic Trends Project, December 2009, updated July 2013, www.pewhispanic.org/2009/12/11/between-two-worlds-how-young-latinos-come-of-age-in-america.

26. Ibid.

27. U.S. Census Bureau, American Fact Finder, Table S1201: Marital Status 2012, American Community Survey 1-Year Estimates.

28. U.S. Census Bureau, Table FG1: Married Couple Family Groups, by Labor Force Status of Both Spouses, and Race and Hispanic Origin/1 of the Reference Person: 2010.

29. Copen et al., "National Health Statistics Report: First Marriages in the United States: Data from the 2006–2010 National Survey of Family Growth."

30. Vespa, Lewis, and Kreider, "America's Families and Living Arrangements: 2012."

31. Ritchie King, "The Uncomfortable Racial Preferences Revealed

by Online Dating," *Quartz*, November 2013, http://qz.com/149342/the -uncomfortable-racial-preferences-revealed-by-online-dating.

32. Ye Luo, Tracey A. LaPierre, Mary Elizabeth Hughes, and Linda J. Waite, "Grandparents Providing Care to Grandchildren: A Population-Based Study of Continuity and Change," *Journal of Family Issues*, April 2012, http://jfi.sagepub.com/content/early/2012/04/18/0192513X124386 85.full.pdf+html.

33. Pew Research Center, "At Grandmother's House We Stay: One-in-Ten Children Are Living with a Grandparent," September 2013, www.pew socialtrends.org/files/2013/09/grandparents_report_final_2013.pdf.

34. Ibid.

35. Ibid.

36. ChildStats.gov, Table FAM1.B: Family Structure and Children's Living Arrangements: Detailed Living Arrangements of Children by Gender, Race and Hispanic Origin, Age, Parent's Education, and Poverty Status, 2012, www.childstats.gov/americaschildren/tables/fam1b.asp?popup=true.

37. Daniel Heimpel, "Americanization, Latino Families and the Future of Foster Care," Chronicle of Social Change, April 2013, https:// chronicleofsocialchange.org/analysis/americanization-latino-families -and-the-future-of-foster-care/2545.

38. Emily Putnam-Hornstein, Barbara Needell, Bryn King, and Michelle Johnson-Motoyama, "Racial and Ethnic Disparities: A Population-Based Examination of Risk Factors for Involvement with Child Protective Services," *Child Abuse and Neglect*, January 2013, www.sciencedirect.com /science/article/pii/S0145213412002190.

39. Sharon Vandivere, Karin Malm, and Laura Radel, "Adoption USA: A Chartbook Based on the 2007 National Survey of Adoptive Parents," U.S. Department of Health and Human Services, last updated 2009, www.aspe .hhs.gov/hsp/09/NSAP/chartbook/chartbook.cfm?id=15.

40. Ibid.

41. Robert P. Jones, Daniel Cox, and Juhem Navarro-Rivera, "How Shifting Religious Identities and Experiences Are Influencing Hispanic Approaches to Politics," Public Religion Research Institute," September 2013, http://publicreligion.org/site/wp-content/uploads/2013/09/2013_HVS _FINAL.pdf.

42. Ibid.

43. Ibid.

44. Paul Taylor, Mark Hugo Lopez, Jessica Martínez, and Gabriel Velasco, "When Labels Don't Fit: Hispanics and Their Views of Identity," Pew Research, Hispanic Trends Project, April 2012, www.pewhispanic .org/2012/04/04/v-politics-values-and-religion.

45. Jones, Cox, and Navarro-Rivera, "How Shifting Religious Identities and Experiences Are Influencing Hispanic Approaches to Politics."

46. Adrianna Quintero-Somaini, Mayra Quirindongo, Evelyn Arévalo, Daniel Lashof, Erik Olson, and Gina Solomon, "Hidden Danger: Environmental Health Threats in the Latino Community," National Resources Defense Council, October 2004, www.nrdc.org/health/effects/latino/english /latino_en.pdf.

47. Paul Taylor and Richard Fry, "The Rise of Residential Segre-

gation by Income," Pew Research Center, Social and Demographic Trends, August 2012, www.pewsocialtrends.org/files/2012/08/Rise-of -Residential-Income-Segregation-2012.2.pdf.

48. Ibid.
49. Ibid.
50. Ibid.
51. Ibid.
52. Ibid.
53. Ibid.
54. Insight Tr3s Newsletter, "Hispanic Millennials: How They Feel About Traditional Food and Cooking," 2012, www.insidetr3s.com /hispanic-millennials-how-they-feel-about-traditional-foods-and-cooking.
55. Nielsen Company, "Popcorn People: Profiles of the U.S. Moviegoer Audience," January 2013, www.nielsen.com/us/en/newswire/2013/popcorn -people-profiles-of-the-u-s-moviegoer-audience.html.
56. Insight Tr3s, "How Hispanic Adult Millennials Spend Their Time," Viacom Entertainment Networks, 2012, www.insidetr3s.com/insight-tr3s /how-hispanic-adult-millennials-spend-their-time.
57. Federal Interagency Forum on Child and Family Statistics, "America's Children: Key National Indicators of Well-Being, 2013."
58. Elizabeth Mendes, "U.S. Blacks', Hispanics' Life Satisfaction up from 2008: Blacks Only Group to Become More Likely to Be Very Satisfied with Lives," Gallup, July 2013, www.gallup.com/poll/163688/blacks-hispanics -life-satisfaction-2008.aspx.
59. Trevor Tompson and Jennifer Benz, "The Public Mood: White Malaise but Optimism Among Blacks, Hispanics," Associated Press and NORC, July 2013, www.apnorc.org/PDFs/Public Mood/AP-NORC_Public MoodWhiteMalaiseButOptimismAmongBlacksandHispanics.pdf.

YOUTH AND EDUCATION

1. U.S. Census Bureau, "Educational Attainment in the United States: 2013" (CPS 2013), www.census.gov/hhes/socdemo/education.
2. Ibid.
3. Ibid.
4. Elizabeth M. Grieco, Yesenia D. Acosta, G. Patricia de la Cruz, Christine Gambino, Thomas Gryn, Luke J. Larsen, Edward N. Trevelyan, and Nathan P. Walters, "The Foreign-Born Population in the United States: 2010," U.S. Census Bureau, May 2012, www.census.gov/prod/2012pubs/acs-19 .pdf.
5. Richard Fry and Mark Hugo Lopez, "Hispanic Student Enrollments Reach New Highs in 2011," Pew Research, Hispanic Trends Project, August 2012, www.pewhispanic.org/2012/08/20/hispanic-student -enrollments-reach-new-highs-in-2011.
6. Ibid.
7. Ibid.
8. Ibid.
9. Ibid.
10. Ibid.
11. Ibid.

12. Ibid.

13. National Center for Education Statistics, "Higher Education: Gaps in Access and Persistence Study: Figure 11-1: Percentage of 9th-Grade Students Who Had Ever Been Retained in Any of Grades Kindergarten Through 9, by Race/Ethnicity and Sex, 2009," 2012, http://nces.ed.gov/pubs2012/2012046/figures/figure_11-1.asp.

14. Ibid.

15. Fry and Lopez, "Hispanic Student Enrollments Reach New Highs in 2011."

16. Ibid.

17. National Center for Education Statistics, "Fast Facts: Dropout Rates," 2013, http://nces.ed.gov/FastFacts/display.asp?id=16; The dropout rate reported here is what is known as the status dropout rate, the percentage of sixteen through twenty-four year olds not enrolled in school and who have not earned a high school diploma or GED certificate.

18. Ibid.

19. Fry and Lopez, "Hispanic Student Enrollments Reach New Highs in 2011."

20. National Center for Education Statistics. "Fast Facts: Dropout Rates."

21. National Center for Education Statistics, "Higher Education: Gaps in Access and Persistence Study: Chapter 3: Student Behaviors and After-school Activities: Indicator 15: Part-Time Work," 2012, http://nces.ed.gov/pubs2012/2012046/chapter3_5.asp.

22. Ibid.

23. Stephanie Ewert, "The Decline in Private School Enrollment," SEHSD Working Paper Number FY12-117, U.S. Census Bureau, January 2013, www.census.gov/hhes/school/files/ewert_private_school_enrollment.pdf; National Center for Education Statistics," Table 69. Percentage Distribution of Students Enrolled in Private Elementary and Secondary Schools, by School Orientation and Selected Characteristics: Fall 2009," 2012, http://nces.ed.gov/programs/digest/d12/tables/dt12_069.asp.

24. Fry and Lopez, "Hispanic Student Enrollments Reach New Highs in 2011."

25. Ibid.

26. Ibid.

27. Ibid.

28. Ibid.

29. Ibid.

30. Ibid.

31. Ibid.

32. Ibid.

33. National Center for Education Statistics, "Fast Facts: Degrees Conferred by Sex and Race," 2013, http://nces.ed.gov/FastFacts/display.asp?id=72.

34. Ibid.

35. Ibid.

36. Gary Orfield, John Kucsera, and Genevieve Siegel-Hawley, "E Pluribus . . . Separation: Deepening Double Segregation for More Students,"

Civil Rights Project, September 2012, http://civilrightsproject.ucla.edu /research/k-12-education/integration-and-diversity/mlk-national/e -pluribus...separation-deepening-double-segregation-for-more-students /orfield_epluribus_revised_omplete_2012.pdf.

37. Ibid.

38. Ibid.

39. National Clearinghouse for English Language Acquisition and Language Instruction Educational Programs, "NCELA Fact Sheet: What Languages Do English Learners Speak?," November 2011, www.ncela.us/files /uploads/NCELAFactsheets/EL_Languages_2011.pdf.

40. Ibid.

41. National Center for Education Statistics, "Mega-States: An Analysis of Student Performance in the Five Most Heavily Populated States in the Nation," February 2013, http://nces.ed.gov/nationsreportcard/pdf /main2011/2013450.pdf.

42. National Center for Education Statistics, "Table 142. Average National Assessment of Educational Progress (NAEP) Reading Scale Score, by Grade and Selected Student and School Characteristics: Selected Years, 1992 through 2011," 2012, https://nces.ed.gov/programs/digest/d12 /tables/dt12_142.asp.

43. Office for Civil Rights, U.S. Department of Education, "The Transformed Civil Rights Data Collection (CRDC)," March 2012, www2.ed.gov /about/offices/list/ocr/docs/crdc-2012-data-summary.pdf.

44. National Center for Education Statistics, "Mega-States: An Analysis of Student Performance in the Five Most Heavily Populated States in the Nation."

45. Ibid.

46. Ibid.

47. Ibid.

48. Ibid.

49. National Center for Education Statistics, "Fast Facts: SAT Scores," 2013, http://nces.ed.gov/fastfacts/display.asp?id=171.

50. Ibid.

51. Ibid.

52. Simone Robers, Jana Kemp, Jennifer Truman, and Thomas D. Snyder, "Indicators of School Crime and Safety: 2012" (NCES 2013-036/NCJ 241446), National Center for Education Statistics, U.S. Department of Education, and Bureau of Justice Statistics, Office of Justice Programs, U.S. Department of Justice, June 2013, http://nces.ed.gov/pubs2013/2013036 .pdf.

53. Ibid.

54. Ibid.

55. Ibid.

56. Ibid.

57. Ibid.

58. Ibid.

59. Office for Civil Rights, U.S. Department of Education, "The Transformed Civil Rights Data Collection (CRDC)."

60. Ibid.

61. Ibid.

62. Ibid.

63. Terris Ross, Grace Kena, Amy Rathbun, Angelina Kewal Ramani, Jijun Zhang, Paul Kristapovich, and Eileen Manning, "Higher Education: Gaps in Access and Persistence Study" (NCES 2012-046), U.S. Department of Education and National Center for Education Statistics, August 2012, http://nces.ed.gov/pubs2012/2012046.pdf.

64. Ibid.

65. Child Trends Data Bank, "Parental Involvement in Schools, Indicators on Children and Youth," September 2013, www.childtrends.org/wp-content/uploads/2012/10/39_Parent_Involvement_In_Schools.pdf.

66. National Center for Education Statistics, Fast Facts, Teacher Trends, http://nces.ed.gov/fastfacts/display.asp?id=28.

67. Ibid.

68. Office for Civil Rights, U.S. Department of Education, "The Transformed Civil Rights Data Collection (CRDC)."

69. Amy Bitterman, Rebecca Goldring, Lucinda Gray, and Stephen Broughman, "Characteristics of Public and Private Elementary and Secondary School Principals in the United States: Results from the 2011–12 Schools and Staffing Survey (NCES 2013-313)" National Center for Education Statistics, U.S. Department of Education, August 2013, http://nces.ed.gov/pubs2013/2013313.pdf .

HEALTH AND ENVIRONMENT

1. Elizabeth Arias, "United States Life Tables, 2008," National Vital Statistics Reports, Vol. 61, No. 3, National Center for Health Statistics, September 2012, www.cdc.gov/nchs/data/nvsr/nvsr61/nvsr61_03.pdf.

2. U.S. Department of Health and Human Services, Office of Minority Health, "Asian American Profile," http://minorityhealth.hhs.gov/templates/browse.aspx?lvl=2&lvlID=53.

3. Donna L. Hoyert and Jiaquan Xu, "Deaths: Preliminary Data for 2011," National Vital Statistics Reports, Vol. 61, No. 6, National Center for Health Statistics, October 2012, www.cdc.gov/nchs/data/nvsr/nvsr61/nvsr61_06.pdf.

4. T.J. Mathews and Marian F. MacDorman, "Infant Mortality Statistics from the 2009 Period: Linked Birth/Infant Death Data Set," National Vital Statistics Reports, Vol. 61, No. 8, National Center for Health Statistics, January 2013, www.cdc.gov/nchs/data/nvsr/nvsr61/nvsr61_08.pdf.

5. Ibid.

6. Gretchen Livingston, Susan Minushkin, and D'Vera Cohn, "Hispanics and Health Care in the United States: Access, Information and Knowledge," Pew Research, Hispanic Trends Project, August 2008, www.pewhispanic.org/2008/08/13/hispanics-and-health-care-in-the-united-states-access-information-and-knowledge.

7. Ibid.

8. U.S. Department of Health and Human Services, Office of Minority Health, "Hispanic/Latino Profile," last updated September 2012, http://minorityhealth.hhs.gov/templates/browse.aspx?lvl=2&lvlID=54.

9. Livingston, Minushkin, and Cohn, "Hispanics and Health Care in the United States: Access, Information and Knowledge."

10. Ibid.

11. Jennifer K. Benz, Valerie A. Welsh, Oscar J. Espinosa, Angela Fontes, Margrethe Montgomery, Nichole Machata, and Garth N. Graham, "Trends in U.S. Public Awareness of Racial and Ethnic Health Disparities (1999–2010,)" U.S. Department of Health and Human Services, Office of Minority Health, September 2010, http://minorityhealth.hhs.gov/assets/pdf/checked/1/2010StudyBrief.pdf.

12. U.S. Department of Health and Human Services, Office of Minority Health, "Obesity and Hispanic Americans," last updated October 2013, http://minorityhealth.hhs.gov/templates/content.aspx?ID=6459; U.S. Department of Health and Human Services, Office of Minority Health, "Obesity and African Americans," last updated October 2013, http://minorityhealth.hhs.gov/templates/content.aspx?ID=6456.

13. U.S. Department of Health and Human Services, Office of Minority Health, "Obesity and Hispanic Americans."

14. Ibid.

15. Ibid.

16. U.S. Department of Health and Human Services, Office of Minority Health, "Heart Disease and Hispanic Americans," last updated August 2012, http://minorityhealth.hhs.gov/templates/content.aspx?ID=3325; U.S. Department of Health and Human Services, Office of Minority Health, "Heart Disease and African Americans," http://minorityhealth.hhs.gov/templates/content.aspx?ID=3018.

17. Ibid.

18. Lisa M. Powell, Sandy Slater, Donka Mirtcheva, Yanjun Bao, and Frank J. Chaloupka, "Food Store Availability and Neighborhood Characteristics in the United States," *Preventive Medicine*, Vol. 44, No. 3, March 2007.

19. Ibid.

20. National Council of La Raza, Profiles of Latino Health, "Issue 4: The Food Environment and Latinos' Access to Healthy Foods," www.nclr.org/images/uploads/pages/Jan12_Profiles_Issue_4.pdf.

21. Ibid.

22. Ibid.

23. U.S. Department of Health and Human Services, Office of Minority Health, "Cancer and Hispanic Americans," last updated June 2012, http://minorityhealth.hhs.gov/templates/content.aspx?lvl=2&lvlID=54&ID=3323; Centers for Disease Control and Prevention, "Cervical Cancer Screening Rates," last updated September 2012, www.cdc.gov/cancer/cervical/statistics/screening.htm.

24. U.S. Department of Health and Human Services, Office of Minority Health, "Heart Disease and Hispanic Americans"; U.S. Department of Health and Human Services, Office of Minority Health, "Heart Disease and African Americans."

25. Ibid.

26. U.S. Department of Health and Human Services, Office of Minority

Health, "Stroke and Hispanic Americans," last updated September 2012, http://minorityhealth.hhs.gov/templates/content.aspx?ID=3330.

27. Ibid.

28. U.S. Department of Health and Human Services, Office of Minority Health, "Diabetes and Hispanic Americans," last updated March 2013, http://minorityhealth.hhs.gov/templates/content.aspx?ID=3324.

29. Ibid.

30. U.S. Department of Health and Human Services, Office of Minority Health, "Asthma and Hispanic Americans," last updated August 2013, http://minorityhealth.hhs.gov/templates/content.aspx?ID=6173.

31. Ibid.

32. Ibid.

33. U.S. Department of Health and Human Services, Office of Minority Health, "HIV/AIDS and Hispanic Americans," last updated August 2013, http://minorityhealth.hhs.gov/templates/content.aspx?ID=3327.

34. Ibid; U.S. Department of Health and Human Services, Office of Minority Health, "HIV/AIDS and African Americans."

35. Ibid.

36. Ibid.

37. Ibid.

38. U.S. Census Bureau, American Fact Finder, "Disability Characteristics: 2012 American Community Survey 1-Year Estimates," Table S1810, http://factfinder2.census.gov/faces/tableservices/jsf/pages/productview .xhtml?pid=ACS_12_1YR_S1810&prodType=table; the Bureau's disability definition encompasses hearing, vision, cognitive, ambulatory, self-care, and independent living difficulties.

39. Centers for Disease Control and Prevention, "Health Disparities in HIV/AIDS, Viral Hepatitis, STDs, and TB: Hispanics/Latinos," last updated September 2013, www.cdc.gov/nchhstp/healthdisparities/Hispanics.html.

40. Ibid.

41. Anjani Chandra, William D. Mosher, Casey Copen, and Catlainn Sionean, "Sexual Behavior, Sexual Attraction, and Sexual Identity in the United States: Data from the 2006–2008 National Survey of Family Growth," National Health Statistics Reports, No. 36, Centers for Disease Control and Prevention, March 2011, www.cdc.gov/nchs/data/nhsr/nhsr036.pdf.

42. Ibid.

43. Ibid.

44. Ibid.

45. Centers for Disease Control and Prevention, "Youth Risk Behavior Surveillance—United States, 2011," Morbidity and Mortality Weekly Report, June 2012, www.cdc.gov/mmwr/pdf/ss/ss6104.pdf.

46. Kimberly Daniels, William D. Mosher, and Jo Jones, "Contraceptive Methods Women Have Ever Used: United States, 1982–2010," National Health Statistics Report, No. 62, February 2013, Centers for Disease Control and Prevention, www.cdc.gov/nchs/data/nhsr/nhsr062.pdf.

47. Anjani Chandra, Veena G. Billioux, Casey E. Copen, and Catlainn Sionean, "HIV Risk-Related Behaviors in the United States Household Population Aged 15–44 Years: Data from the National Survey of Family

Growth, 2002 and 2006–2010," National Health Statistics Report, No. 46, Centers for Disease Control and Prevention, January 2012, www.cdc.gov /nchs/data/nhsr/nhsr046.pdf.

48. Brady E. Hamilton, Joyce A. Martin, and Stephanie J. Ventura, "Births: Preliminary Data for 2011," National Vital Statistics Reports, Vol. 61, No. 5, Centers for Disease Control and Prevention, October 2012, www.cdc.gov/nchs/data/nvsr/nvsr61/nvsr61_05.pdf.

49. Joyce A. Martin, Brady E. Hamilton, Stephanie J. Ventura, Michelle J.K. Osterman, and T.J. Mathews, "Births: Final Data for 2011," National Vital Statistics Reports, June 2013, Centers for Disease Control and Prevention, www.cdc.gov/nchs/data/nvsr/nvsr62/nvsr62_01.pdf.

50. Brady E. Hamilton, T.J. Mathews, and Stephanie J. Ventura, "Declines in State Teen Birth Rates by Race and Hispanic Origin," NCHA Data Brief, No. 123, Centers for Disease Control and Prevention, May 2013, www.cdc.gov/nchs/data/databriefs/db123.pdf.

51. Ibid.

52. Brady E. Hamilton, Joyce A. Martin, and Stephanie J. Ventura, "Births: Preliminary Data for 2011," National Vital Statistics Reports, Vol. 61, No. 5, Centers for Disease Control and Prevention, October 2012, www.cdc.gov/nchs/data/nvsr/nvsr61/nvsr61_05.pdf.

53. Ibid.

54. Daniels, Mosher, and Jones, "Contraceptive Methods Women Have Ever Used: United States, 1982–2012."

55. Ibid.

56. Guttmacher Institute, "Fact Sheet: Induced Abortions in the United States," December 2013, updated July 2014, www.guttmacher.org/pubs /fb_induced_abortion.html; Centers for Disease Control and Prevention, "Health Disparities in HIV/AIDS, Viral Hepatitis, STDs, and TB: Hispanics/ Latinos."

57. Paul Taylor, Mark Hugo Lopez, Jessica Martínez, and Gabriel Velasco, "When Labels Don't Fit: Hispanics and Their Views of Identity," Pew Research, Hispanic Trends Project, April 2012, www.pewhispanic.org/2012/04 /04/when-labels-dont-fit-hispanics-and-their-views-of-identity.

58. Ibid.

59. Luis R. Fraga, John A. Garcia, Rodney E. Hero, Michael Jones-Correa, Valerie Marinez-Ebers, and Gary M. Segura, Latinos in the New Millennium (New York: Cambridge University Press, 2012).

60. Planned Parenthood, "New Poll of Latinos in the U.S. Shows Overwhelming Support for Sex Education and Access to Birth Control to Reduce Teen Pregnancy," April 2013, www.plannedparenthood.org/about-us /newsroom/press-releases/new-poll-latinos-us-shows-overwhelming -support-sex-education-access-birth-control-reduce-teen-p-41236.htm.

61. U.S. Department of Health and Human Services, Office of Minority Health, "Mental Health and Hispanics," last updated December 2012, http://minorityhealth.hhs.gov/templates/content.aspx?ID=6477.

62. Amy M. Bauer, Chih-Nan Chen, and Margarita Alegría, "English Language Proficiency and Mental Health Service Use Among Latino and Asian Americans with Mental Disorders," Med Care, December 2011, www.ncbi .nlm.nih.gov/pmc/articles/PMC3135417.

63. U.S. Department of Health and Human Services, Office of Minority Health, "Mental Health and Hispanics."

64. Ibid.

65. Centers for Disease Control and Prevention, "Youth Risk Behavior Surveillance—United States, 2011."

66. Substance Abuse and Mental Health Services Administration, Office of Applied Studies, "The NSDUH Report: Substance Use Among Hispanic Adults," June 2010, www.oas.samhsa.gov/2k10/184/HispanicAdults.pdf.

67. Ibid.

68. Ibid.

69. Laura Castillo-Page, "Diversity in Medical Education: Facts and Figures 2012," Association of American Medical Colleges, 2012, https://members.aamc.org/eweb/upload/Diversity%20in%20Medical%20Education_Facts%20and%20Figures%202012.pdf

70. Health Resources and Services Administration, Bureau of Health Professions, National Center for Health Workforce Analysis, "The U.S. Nursing Workforce: Trends in Supply and Education," April 2013, http://bhpr.hrsa.gov/healthworkforce/reports/nursingworkforce/nursingworkforcefullreport.pdf.

71. Adrianna Quintero-Somaini, Mayra Quirindongo, Evelyn Arévalo, Daniel Lashof, Erik Olson, and Gina Solomon, "Hidden Danger: Environmental Health Threats in the Latino Community," National Resources Defense Council, October 2004, www.nrdc.org/health/effects/latino/english/latino_en.pdf.

72. Ibid.

73. Ibid.

74. Ibid.

75. Ibid.

76. Ibid.

77. Sierra Club and National Council of La Raza, "2012 National Latinos and the Environment Survey," 2012, www.sierraclub.org/ecocentro/survey/2012%20Latinos%20and%20the%20Environment%20Survey_Exec%20Summary_English.pdf.

78. Ibid.

79. Ibid.

CRIMINAL JUSTICE

1. California Department of Justice, "Crime in California, 2012," July 2013, http://oag.ca.gov/sites/all/files/agweb/pdfs/cjsc/publications/candd/cd12/cd12.pdf.

2. Texas Department of Public Safety, "Chapter 9: 2012 Texas Arrest Data," in 2012 Crime in Texas, 2012, www.dps.texas.gov/crimereports/12/citCh9.pdf.

3. Lynda Garcia, "The War on Marijuana Has a Latino Data Problem," American Civil Liberties Union, June 2013, www.aclu.org/blog/criminal-law-reform-racial-justice/war-marijuana-has-latino-data-problem.

4. Mark Hugo Lopez and Gretchen Livingston, "Hispanics and the Criminal Justice System: Low Confidence, High Exposure," Pew Research,

Hispanic Trends Project, April 2009, www.pewhispanic.org/2009/04/07 /hispanics-and-the-criminal-justice-system.

5. Lynn Langton and Matthew Durose, "Police Behavior During Traffic and Street Stops, 2011," Bureau of Justice Statistics, September 2013, www.bjs.gov/content/pub/pdf/pbtss11.pdf.

6. Rich Morin, "Crime Rises Among Second-Generation Immigrants as They Assimilate," Pew Research Center, October 2013, www .pewresearch.org/fact-tank/2013/10/15/crime-rises-among-second -generation-immigrants-as-they-assimilate.

7. Ibid.

8. California Department of Justice, "Crime in California, 2012."

9. Marguerite Moeller, "Latino Youth in the Juvenile Justice System," National Council of La Raza, March 2011, www.nclr.org/images/uploads /publications/Latino_Youth_in_the_Juvenile_Justice_System.pdf.

10. Jennifer Truman, Lynn Langton, and Michael Planty, "Criminal Victimization, 2012," Bureau of Justice Statistics, October 2013, www.bjs.gov /content/pub/pdf/cv12.pdf.

11. Jennifer Hardison Walters, Andrew Moore, Marcus Berzofsky, and Lynn Langton, "Household Burglary, 1994–2011," Bureau of Justice Statistics, June 2013, www.bjs.gov/content/pub/pdf/hb9411.pdf.

12. Centers for Disease Control and Prevention, "10 Leading Causes of Death, United States 2010, All Races, Hispanic, Both Sexes," last updated February 2013, available via http://webappa.cdc.gov/sasweb/ncipc /leadcaus10_us.html.

13. Federal Bureau of Investigation, "2012 Hate Crime Statistics: Victims," www.fbi.gov/about-us/cjis/ucr/hate-crime/2012/topic-pages/victims /victims_final.

14. American Bar Association, Commission on Hispanic Legal Rights and Responsibilities, "Latinos in the United States: Overcoming Legal Obstacles, Engaging in Civic Life," 2013, www.americanbar.org/content/dam /aba/images/commission_on_hispanic_legal_rights_responsibilities /hispanicreportnew.pdf.

15. Erika Harrell and Lynn Langton, "Victims of Identity Theft, 2012," Bureau of Justice Statistics, December 2013, www.bjs.gov/content/pub /pdf/vit12.pdf.

16. Lopez and Livingston, "Hispanics and the Criminal Justice System: Low Confidence, High Exposure,"

17. Ibid.

18. Ibid.

19. Ibid.

20. Ibid.

21. Ibid.

22. Ibid.

23. Ibid.

24. Ibid.

25. Ibid.

26. Lynn Langton and Matthew Durose, "Police Behavior During Traffic and Street Stops, 2011."

27. New York Civil Liberties Union, "Stop-and-Frisk Data," www.nyclu
.org/content/stop-and-frisk-data.

28. Pew Research, Hispanic Trends Project, "Hispanics and Arizona's New Immigration Law: Fact Sheet," April 2010, www.pewhispanic
.org/2010/04/29/hispanics-and-arizonas-new-immigration-law.

29. Bureau of Labor Statistics, "Table 11: Employed Persons by Detailed
Occupation, Sex, Race, and Hispanic or Latino Ethnicity," February 2013,
www.bls.gov/cps/cpsaat11.pdf.

30. Brian A. Reaves, "Local Police Departments, 2007," Bureau of Justice Statistics, December 2010, www.bjs.gov/content/pub/pdf/lpd07.pdf.

31. Federal Bureau of Investigation, "Today's FBI: Facts and Figures
2013–2014," March 2013, www.fbi.gov/stats-services/publications/todays
-fbi-facts-figures/facts-and-figures-031413.pdf/view.

32. U.S. Office of Personnel Management, "Eleventh Annual Report
to the President on Hispanic Employment in the Federal Government,"
July 2012, www.opm.gov/policy-data-oversight/diversity-and-inclusion
/reports/hispanic_july2012.pdf.

33. Anna Brown and Mark Hugo Lopez, "Mapping the Latino Population, by State, County and City: Ranking Latino Populations in the
Nation's Metropolitan Areas," Pew Research, Hispanic Trends Project, August 2013, www.pewhispanic.org/2013/08/29/iv-ranking-latino
-populations-in-the-nations-metropolitan-areas.

34. New York City Police Department, "Crime and Enforcement Activity
in New York City (January to June 2013)," 2013, www.nyc.gov/html/nypd
/downloads/pdf/analysis_and_planning/2012_year_end_enforcement
_report.pdf.

35. U.S. Department of Justice, Civil Rights Division, "Investigation of
the Puerto Rico Police Department," September 2011, www.justice.gov
/crt/about/spl/documents/prpd_letter.pdf.

36. U.S. Census Bureau, "Table 616. Employed Civilians by Occupation,
Sex, Race, and Hispanic Origin: 2010," 2012, www.census.gov/compendia
/statab/2012/tables/12s0616.pdf.

37. Jill L. Cruz, Melinda S. Molina, and Jenny Rivera, "La Voz De La
Abogada Latina: Challenges and Rewards in Serving the Public Interest,"
Hispanic National Bar Association Commission on the Status of Latinas
in the Legal Profession, September 2010, http://198.171.230.232/files
/warehouse_attachment_1399880167.pdf.

38. American Bar Association, Commission on Hispanic Legal Rights
and Responsibilities, "Latinos in the United States: Overcoming Legal Obstacles, Engaging in Civic Life."

39. Ibid.

40. U.S. Office of Personnel Management, "Eleventh Annual Report to
the President on Hispanic Employment in the Federal Government."

41. Association of American Law Schools, "Statistical Report on Law
School Faculty and Candidates for Law Faculty Positions, 2008–2009,"
www.aals.org/statistics/2009dlt/gender.html.

42. Glenn R. Schmitt and Jennifer Dukes, "Overview of Federal Criminal
Cases: Fiscal Year 2012," U.S. Sentencing Commission, 2013, www.ussc.

gov/Research_and_Statistics/Research_Publications/2013/FY12_Over
view_Federal_Criminal_Cases.pdf.

43. Ibid.

44. E. Ann Carson and Daniela Golinelli, "Prisoners in 2012—Advance Counts," Bureau of Justice Statistics, July 2013, www.bjs.gov/content/pub/pdf/p12ac.pdf.

45. Ibid.

46. Ibid.

47. Sourcebook of Criminal Justice Statistics, "Table 6.33.2010: Estimated Number and Rate (per 100,000 U.S. Resident Population in Each Group) of Sentenced Prisoners Under Jurisdiction of State and Federal Correctional Authorities," 2010, www.albany.edu/sourcebook/pdf/t6332010.pdf.

48. The Sentencing Project, "Fact Sheet: Trends in U.S. Corrections," updated April 2014, http://sentencingproject.org/doc/publications/inc_Trends_in_Corrections_Fact_sheet.pdf.

49. Sourcebook of Criminal Justice Statistics, "Table 6.33.2010: Estimated Number and Rate (per 100,000 U.S. Resident Population in Each Group) of Sentenced Prisoners Under Jurisdiction of State and Federal Correctional Authorities."

50. National Center for Juvenile Justice, *Easy Access to the Census of Juveniles in Residential Placement: 1997–2011*, Office of Juvenile Justice and Delinquency Prevention, www.ojjdp.gov/ojstatbb/ezacjrp/asp/Offense_Race.asp.

51. Marguerite Moeller, "Latino Youth in the Juvenile Justice System," National Council of La Raza, March 2011, www.nclr.org/images/uploads/publications/Latino_Youth_in_the_Juvenile_Justice_System.pdf.

52. Ibid.

53. National Center for Juvenile Justice, *Easy Access to the Census of Juveniles in Residential Placement: 1997–2011*, Office of Juvenile Justice and Delinquency Prevention, http://www.ojjdp.gov/ojstatbb/ezacjrp/asp/Offense_Race.asp.

54. Ibid.

55. José D. Saavedra, "Just the Facts: A Snapshot of Incarcerated Hispanic Youth," National Council of La Raza, March 2010, www.nclr.org/index.php/publications/just_the_facts_a_snapshot_of_incarcerated_hispanic_youth.

56. Ibid.

57. Allen J. Beck, Marcus Berzofsky, Rachel Caspar, and Christopher Krebs, "Sexual Victimization in Prisons and Jails Reported by Inmates, 2011–12," Bureau of Justice Statistics, May 2013, www.bjs.gov/content/pub/pdf/svpjri1112.pdf.

58. Allen J. Beck, David Cantor, John Hartge, and Tim Smith, "Sexual Victimization in Juvenile Facilities Reported by Youth, 2012," Bureau of Justice Statistics, June 2013, www.bjs.gov/content/pub/pdf/svjfry12.pdf.

59. Deborah Fins, "Death Row U.S.A., Spring 2013," NAACP Legal Defense and Educational Fund, Inc., April 2013, www.naacpldf.org/files/publications/DRUSA_Spring_2013.pdf.

60. Ibid.

61. Ibid.
62. Deborah Fins, "Death Row U.S.A., Spring 2013."
63. E. Ann Carson and Daniela Golinelli, "Prisoners in 2012—Advance Counts," Bureau of Justice Statistics, July 2013, www.bjs.gov/content/pub/pdf/p12ac.pdf.
64. Mark Motivans, "Federal Justice Statistics, 2009," Bureau of Justice Statistics, December 2011, www.bjs.gov/content/pub/pdf/fjs09.pdf.
65. Ibid.
66. Ibid.
67. National Gang Center, *National Youth Gang Survey Analysis: Race/Ethnicity of Gang Members 1996–2011,* www.nationalgangcenter.gov/Survey-Analysis/Demographics#anchorregm.
68. Pew Research, Hispanic Trends Project, "Between Two Worlds: How Young Latinos Come of Age in America," December 2009, updated July 2013, www.pewhispanic.org/2009/12/11/between-two-worlds-how-young-latinos-come-of-age-in-america/.
69. Glenn R. Schmitt and Jennifer Dukes, "Overview of Federal Criminal Cases: Fiscal Year 2012," United States Sentencing Commission, 2013, www.ussc.gov/Research_and_Statistics/Research_Publications/2013/FY12_Overview_Federal_Criminal_Cases.pdf.
70. John Simanski and Lesley M. Sapp, "Immigration Enforcement Actions: 2011," Department of Homeland Security Office of Immigration Statistics, September 2012, www.dhs.gov/sites/default/files/publications/immigration-statistics/enforcement_ar_2011.pdf.
71. Ibid.
72. Motivans, "Federal Justice Statistics, 2009."
73. Ibid.
74. Simanski and Sapp, "Immigration Enforcement Actions: 2011."

ENTERTAINMENT, TECHNOLOGY, AND SPORTS

1. Nielsen Company, "Popcorn People: Profiles of the U.S. Moviegoer Audience," January 2013, www.nielsen.com/us/en/newswire/2013/popcorn-people-profiles-of-the-u-s-moviegoer-audience.html.
2. Ibid.
3. Jorge Rivas, "Summer Hit Movie Surprises Everyone Except Mexicans," *Fusion,* September 2013, http://fusion.net/culture/story/spanglish-film-instructions-included-breaks-records-17744.
4. Mark Hughes, "Latino Site Launches Film Project as Latino Audiences Flex Box Office Muscle," *Forbes,* June 2013, www.forbes.com/sites/markhughes/2013/06/29/latino-site-launches-film-project-as-latino-audiences-flex-box-office-muscle/.
5. Sam Thielman, "Hispanic Networks Bring in Auto Dollars in a Weak Year for Broadcast Telemundo and Univision Write Increases," *AdWeek,* June 2013, www.adweek.com/news/television/hispanic-networks-bring-auto-dollars-weak-year-broadcast-150669.
6. Mark Hugo Lopez, "What Univision's Milestone Says About U.S. Demographics," Pew Research, Hispanic Trends Project, July 2013, www.pewresearch.org/fact-tank/2013/07/29/what-univisions-milestone-says-about-u-s-demographics.

7. Univision Communications, "'Despierta America' Concludes Season with Best Viewership in the History of the Show," October 2013, http://corporate.univision.com/2013/press/despierta-america-concludes-season-with-best-viewership-in-the-history-of-the-show/#axzz2mx2ak AUU.

8. Ibid.

9. Ibid.

10. Meg James, "Univision Morning Show May Be an Awakening for Big Networks," *Los Angeles Times*, July 2013, www.latimes.com/entertainment/envelope/cotown/la-fi-ct-despierta-america-20130702,0,5473907.story#axzz2n6bAso9i.

11. Lopez, "What Univision's Milestone Says About U.S. Demographics."

12. Matt A. Barreto, Sylvia Manzano, and Gary Segura, "The Impact of Media Stereotypes on Opinions and Attitudes Towards Latinos," National Hispanic Media Coalition and Latino Decisions, September 2012, www.chicano.ucla.edu/files/news/NHMCLatinoDecisionsReport.pdf.

13. Mark Hugo Lopez and Ana Gonzalez-Barrera, "A Growing Share of Latinos Get Their News in English," Pew Research, Hispanic Trends Project, July 2013, www.pewhispanic.org/2013/07/23/a-growing-share-of-latinos-get-their-news-in-english.

14. Ibid.

15. Ibid.

16. Ibid.

17. Ibid.

18. Ibid.

19. "Hispanic Fact Pack 2013: Advertising Age's Annual Guide to Hispanic Marketing and Media," Ad Age Data Center, July 2013, http://adage.com/trend-reports/report.php?id=78.

20. Lopez and Gonzalez-Barrera, "A Growing Share of Latinos Get Their News in English."

21. Ibid.

22. Ibid.

23. Ibid.

24. Nielsen Company, "A Look Across Media: the Cross-Platform Report, December 2013," December 2013, www.nielsen.com/content/dam/corporate/us/en/reports-downloads/2013%20Reports/The-Cross-Platform-Report-A-Look-Across-Media-3Q2013.pdf.

25. Ibid.

26. Ibid.

27. "Hispanic Fact Pack 2013: Advertising Age's Annual Guide to Hispanic Marketing and Media."

28. Ibid.

29. Nielsen Company, "A Snapshot of Hispanic Media Usage in the U.S.," September 2010, www.nielsen.com/content/dam/corporate/us/en/reports-downloads/2010-Reports/Nielsen-Snapshot-of-Hispanic-Media-Usage-US.pdf.

30. Nielsen Company, "State of the Hispanic Consumer: The Hispanic Market Imperative," 2012, www.nielsen.com/content/dam/corporate/us

/en/reports-downloads/2012-Reports/State-of-the-Hispanic-Consumer
.pdf.

31. Nielsen Company, "A Look Across Media: the Cross-Platform Report, December 2013," December 2013, www.nielsen.com/content/dam
/corporate/us/en/reports-downloads/2013%20Reports/The-Cross
-Platform-Report-A-Look-Across-Media-3Q2013.pdf.

32. Ibid.

33. Nielsen Company, "How the Hispanic Consumer Is Influencing the
Entertainment Industry," September 2013, www.nielsen.com/us/en/news
wire/2013/how-the-hispanic-consumer-is-influencing-the-entertainment
-indus.html.

34. Univision Communications, *U.S. Hispanics: the Ultimate Social Powerhouse*, 2013, http://corporate.univision.com/wp-content/uploads/2013/11
/US_Hispanics_The_Ultimate_Social_Powerhouse_Infographic2.jpg.

35. Insight Tr3s, "Who's Listening to Latin Music? And What Are
They Listening To?," Viacom International Media Networks, November
2013, www.insidetr3s.com/insight-tr3s/whos-listening-to-latin-music-and
-what-are-they-listening-to.

36. Dorothy Pomerantz, "J.Lo's Stunning Career Reincarnation Puts
Her No. 1 on the Celebrity 100," *Forbes*, May 2012, www.forbes.com/sites
/dorothypomerantz/2012/05/16/jennifer-lopez-tops-celebrity-100-list.

37. Jonathan Muñoz, "Forbes Most Powerful Latino Celebrities of 2013,"
Voxxi, June 2013, http://voxxi.com/2013/06/26/most-powerful-latino-cele
brities-2013.

38. Meghan Casserly, "Sofia Vergara Is the Top-Earning Actress
on Television . . . by a Longshot," *Forbes*, September 2013, www
.forbes.com/sites/meghancasserly/2013/09/04/sofia-vergara-is-the-top
-earning-actress-on-television-by-a-longshot.

39. Bureau of Labor Statistics, "Table 11: Employed Persons by Detailed
Occupation, Sex, Race, and Hispanic or Latino Ethnicity, 2013," February
2013, www.bls.gov/cps/cpsaat11.pdf.

40. Ibid.

41. Darnell Hunt, "Hollywood Diversity Brief: Spotlight on Cable Television," Ralph J. Bunche Center for African American Studies, University
of California, Los Angeles, October 2013, www.bunchecenter.ucla.edu/wp
-content/uploads/2013/10/Hollywood-Diversity-Brief-Spotlight-10-2013
.pdf.

42. Bureau of Labor Statistics, "Table 11: Employed Persons by Detailed
Occupation, Sex, Race, and Hispanic or Latino Ethnicity, 2013."

43. Writers Guild of America, West, "Writers Guild of America, West,
2013 TV Staffing Brief," 2013, www.wga.org/uploadedFiles/who_we_are
/tvstaffingbrief2013.pdf.

44. Ibid.

45. Stacy L. Smith, Marc Choueiti, and Katherine Pieper, "Race/Ethnicity
in 500 Popular Films: Is the Key to Diversifying Cinematic Content Held in
the Hand of the Black Director?," Media Diversity and Social Change Initiative, University of Southern California, 2013, http://annenberg.usc.edu
/sitecore/shell/Applications/~/media/PDFs/RaceEthnicity.ashx.

46. Matt A. Barreto, Sylvia Manzano, and Gary Segura, "The Impact of Media Stereotypes on Opinions and Attitudes Towards Latinos," National Hispanic Media Coalition and Latino Decisions, September 2012, www .chicano.ucla.edu/files/news/NHMCLatinoDecisionsReport.pdf.

47. Smith, Choueiti, and Pieper, "Race/Ethnicity in 500 Popular Films: Is the Key to Diversifying Cinematic Content Held in the Hand of the Black Director?"

48. Wikipedia.org, *List of Hispanic-American (U.S.) Academy Award Winners and Nominees*, last modified July 2013, http://en.wikipedia.org /wiki/List_of_Hispanic-American_(U.S.)_Academy_Award_winners_and _nominees.

49. Lee Hernandez, "A Look at Latino Emmy Winners over the Years," *Latina*, September 2011, www.latina.com/entertainment/tv/look -latino-emmy-winners-over-years#ixzz2rLOzEAQr.

50. Ibid.

51. Sugey Palomares, "10 Latino Golden Globe Winners!," *Latina*, January 2013, www.latina.com/entertainment/buzz/10-latino-golden-globe -winners.

52. Erica E. Phillips, "Can Latin Grammys Give the Music a Lift?," *Wall Street Journal*, http://online.wsj.com/news/articles/SB10001424127887324 595904578119143177055064.

53. Univision Communications, "14th Annual Latin Grammy® Awards Reaches 9.8 Million Viewers and Makes Univision a Top 3 Network for the Night Among Both Adults 18–49 and Adults 18–34," November 2013, http://corporate.univision.com/2013/press/14th-annual-latin-grammy%C2 %AE-awards-reaches-9-8-million-viewers-and-makes-univision-a-top-3 -network-for-the-night-among-both-adults-18-49-and-adults-18-34/#ax zz2mOUTRHLi.

54. Rick Kissell, "Latin Grammys Rule Ratings in L.A., Dallas and Other Cities," *Variety*, November 2013, http://variety.com/2013/tv/ratings/latin -grammys-rule-ratings-in-l-a-dallas-and-other-cities-1200870417.

55. Ibid.

56. United States Department of Labor, "The Latino Labor Force in the Recovery," April 2012, www.dol.gov/_sec/media/reports/hispaniclabor force.

57. Deborah A. Santiago, "Finding Your Workforce: The Top 25 Institutions Graduating Latinos in Science, Technology, Engineering, and Math (STEM) by Academic Level 2009–2010," Excelencia in Education, July 2012, www.edexcelencia.org/research/finding-your-workforce-top-25-institu tions-graduating-latinos-science-technology.

58. Dan Nakaso, "Asian Workers Now Dominate Silicon Valley Tech Jobs," *San Jose Mercury News*, November 2012, www.mercurynews.com /ci_22094415/asian-workers-now-dominate-silicon-valley-tech-jobs.

59. Yoree Koh, "Twitter Users' Diversity Becomes an Ad Selling Point Microblogging Social-Media Site Trying to Capitalize on Its Demographics," *Wall Street Journal*, January 2014, http://online.wsj.com/news/articles /SB10001424052702304419104579323442346646168?mg=reno64-wsj &url=http%3A%2F%2Fonline.wsj.com%2Farticle%2FSB100014240 52702304419104579323442346646168.html.

60. Mark Hugo Lopez, Ana Gonzalez Barrera, and Eileen Patten, "Closing the Digitial Divide: Latinos and Technology Adoption," Pew Research Center, Hispanic Trends Project, March 7, 2013, www.pewhispanic.org/2013/03 /07/closing-the-digital-divide-latinos-and-technology-adoption.

61. Kathryn Zickuhr and Lee Rainie, "7 Things To Know About Offline Americans," Pew Research Center, November 2013, www.pewresearch .org/fact-tank/2013/11/29/7-things-to-know-about-offline-americans.

62. Nielsen Company, "State of the Hispanic Consumer: The Hispanic Market Imperative."

63. Ibid.

64. Nielsen Company, "A Look Across Media: the Cross-Platform Report, December 2013."

65. Ibid.

66. Ibid.

67. Nielsen Company, "How the Hispanic Consumer Is Influencing the Entertainment Industry," September 2013, www.nielsen.com/us/en/news wire/2013/how-the-hispanic-consumer-is-influencing-the-entertainment -indus.html.

68. Nielsen Company, "State of the Hispanic Consumer: The Hispanic Market Imperative."

69. Nielsen Company, "How the Hispanic Consumer Is Influencing the Entertainment Industry."

70. Nielsen Company, "Latina Power Shift," 2013, www.nielsen.com /content/dam/corporate/us/en/reports-downloads/2013%20Reports /Nielsen-Latina-Report-2013.pdf.

71. "Hispanic Fact Pack 2013: Advertising Age's Annual Guide to Hispanic Marketing and Media."

72. Ibid.

73. Ibid

74. Ibid.

75. Univision Communications, *U.S. Hispanics: the Ultimate Social Powerhouse*, 2013, http://corporate.univision.com/wp-content/uploads/2013 /11/US_Hispanics_The_Ultimate_Social_Powerhouse_Infographic2.jpg.

76. Nielsen Company, "A Look Across Media: the Cross-Platform Report, December 2013."

77. Nielsen Company, "How the Hispanic Consumer Is Influencing the Entertainment Industry."

78. Ibid.

79. Ibid.

80. Ron Rodrigues, "Hispanic Radio Today 2013," Arbitron Inc., 2013, http://www.arbitron.com/downloads/Hispanic_Radio_Today_2013_exec sum.pdf.

81. Inight Tr3s, "Who's Listening to Latin Music? And What Are They Listening To?"

82. Ibid.

83. Rodrigues, "Hispanic Radio Today 2013."

84. Nielsen Company, "How the Hispanic Consumer Is Influencing the Entertainment Industry."

85. Ibid.

86. "Hispanic Fact Pack 2013: Advertising Age's Annual Guide to Hispanic Marketing and Media."

87. Rodrigues, "Hispanic Radio Today 2013."

88. Lee Rainie, Kathryn Zickuhr, Kristen Purcell, Mary Madden, and Joanna Brenner, "The Rise of E-Reading," Pew Research Center, Pew Internet and American Life Project, April 2012, http://libraries.pewinternet.org/files/legacy-pdf/The%20rise%20of%20e-reading%204.5.12.pdf.

89. Ellen Wartella, Emily Kirkpatrick, Victoria Rideout, Alexis R. Lauricella, and Sabrina L. Connell, "Media, Technology, and Reading in Hispanic Families: A National Survey," Center on Media and Human Development at Northwestern University and National Center for Families Learning, December 2013, http://familieslearning.org/PDF/HispanicFamMediaSurvey_Dec13.pdf.

90. Rainie, Zickuhr, Purcell, Madden, and Brenner, "The Rise of E-Reading."

91. Leylha Ahuile, "People of the Book: Spanish-Language Publishing 2013," *Publishers Weekly*, October 2013, www.publishersweekly.com/pw/by-topic/international/international-book-news/article/59640-people-of-the-book-spanish-language-publishing-2013.html.

92. Portada, "'77% of Spanish-Language Books Ever Published Are Available in the U.S.', Says Amazon's Pedro Huerta," October 2013, www.portada-online.com/2013/10/18/77-of-spanish-language-books-ever-published-are-available-in-the-u-s-says-amazons-pedro-huerta/.

93. *Publishers Weekly*, "In the News: Spanish Supplement Spring 2013," March 2013, www.publishersweekly.com/pw/by-topic/international/international-book-news/article/56586-in-the-news-spanish-supplement-spring-2013.html.

94. Pulitzer Prizes administered by Columbia University, *Pulitzer Prize Winners: Fiction*, www.pulitzer.org/bycat/Fiction; MacArthur Fellows Program, MacArthur Foundation, *MacArthur Fellows|Meet the Class of 2012: Junot Díaz*, www.macfound.org/fellows/864/.

95. Wikipedia, *My Beloved World*, http://en.wikipedia.org/wiki/My_Beloved_World.

96. The Nielsen Company, "State of the Hispanic Consumer: The Hispanic Market Imperative," 2012, http://www.nielsen.com/content/dam/corporate/us/en/reports-downloads/2012-Reports/State-of-the-Hispanic-Consumer.pdf

97. Nielsen Company, "State of the Media: 2012 Year in Sports," January 2013, www.nielsen.com/content/corporate/us/en/insights/reports/2013/state-of-the-media--2012-year-in-sports.html.

98. ESPN/ESPN Deportes, *29 Million Fans, 2012*, www.espndeportessales.com/29-million-fans.

99. "Hispanic Fact Pack 2013: Advertising Age's Annual Guide to Hispanic Marketing and Media."

100. Richard Lapchick, Cory Bernstine, Giomar Nunes, Nicole Okolo, Deidre Snively, and Curtis Walker, "The 2013 Racial and Gender Report Card: Major League Baseball," Institute for Diversity and Ethics in Sport, May 2013, www.tidesport.org/RGRC/2013/2013_MLB_RGRC_Final_Correction.pdf.

101. Kurt Badenhausen, "Baseball's Highest-Paid Players on and off the Field," *Forbes*, March 2013, http://www.forbes.com/sites/kurt badenhausen/2013/03/27/baseballs-highest-paid-players-on-and-off -the-field-2/; Jay Jaffe, "Alex Rodriguez Suspended for 162 Games," *Sports Illustrated*, January 2014, http://mlb.si.com/2014/01/11/alex-rodri guez-suspended-for-162-games/.

102. Badenhausen, "Baseball's Highest-Paid Players on and off the Field."

103. Richard Lapchick, Andrew Hippert, and Cory Bernstine, "The 2013 Racial and Gender Report Card: Major League Soccer," Institute for Diversity and Ethics in Sport, November 2013, www.tidesport.org /RGRC/2013/2013_MLS_RGRC.pdf.

104. Richard Lapchick, Andrew Hippert, Stephanie Rivera, and Jason Robinson, "The 2013 Racial and Gender Report Card: National Basketball Association," Institute for Diversity and Ethics in Sport, June 2013, www .tidesport.org/RGRC/2013/2013_NBA_RGRC.pdf.

105. Richard Lapchick, Devin Beahm, Giomar Nunes, and Stephanie Rivera-Casiano, "The 2013 Racial and Gender Report Card: National Football League," Institute for Diversity and Ethics in Sport, October 2013, www.tidesport.org/RGRC/2013/2013_NFL_RGRC.pdf.

106. Richard Lapchick et al., "The 2013 Racial and Gender Report Card: Major League Baseball."

107. Richard Lapchick et al., "The 2013 Racial and Gender Report Card: National Football League."

108. Richard Lapchick et al., "The 2013 Racial and Gender Report Card: Major League Baseball."

109. Richard Lapchick et al., "The 2013 Racial and Gender Report Card: National Football League."

110. Richard Lapchick, Claire Burnett, Michael Farris, Reggie Gossett, Chris Orpilla, James Phelan, Tamara Sherrod, Sean Smith, Steve Thiel, Curtis Walker, and Deidre Snively, "The 2012 Associated Press Sports Editors Racial and Gender Report Card," Institute for Diversity and Ethics in Sport, March 2013, www.tidesport.org/RGRC/2012/2012_APSE_RGRC.pdf.

111. Ibid.

IDENTITY

1. Paul Taylor, Mark Hugo Lopez, Jessica Martínez, and Gabriel Velasco, "When Labels Don't Fit: Hispanics and Their View of Identity," Pew Research, Hispanic Trends Project, April 2012, www.pewhispanic.org/2012/04/04 /when-labels-dont-fit-hispanics-and-their-views-of-identity/.

2. Ibid.

3. Gabriel Sanchez, "Taking a Closer Look at Latino Pan-Ethnic Identity," *Latino Decisions*, April 2012, www.latinodecisions.com/blog /2012/04/18/taking-a-closer-look-at-latino-pan-ethnic-identity; Mark Hugo Lopez, Rich Morin, and Paul Taylor, "Illegal Immigration Backlash Worries, Divides Latinos," Pew Research, Hispanic Trends Project, October 2010, www.pewhispanic.org/2010/10/28/illegal-immigration-backlash-worries -divides-latinos/.

4. Pew Research, Hispanic Trends Project, "Three-Fourths of

Hispanics Say Their Community Needs a Leader," October 2013, www.pewhispanic.org/2013/10/22/three-fourths-of-hispanics-say -their-community-needs-a-leader/ph-hispanic-leader-10-2013-03-03.

5. Mark Hugo Lopez, Ana Gonzalez-Barrera, and Danielle Cuddington, "Diverse Origins: The Nation's 14 Largest Hispanic Origin Groups," Pew Research, Hispanic Trends Project, June 2013, www .pewhispanic.org/2013/06/19/diverse-origins-the-nations-14-largest -hispanic-origin-groups/.

6. Wikipedia, *History of Hispanic and Latino Americans*, http:// en.wikipedia.org/wiki/History_of_Hispanic_and_Latino_Americans.

7. Ibid.

8. Ibid.

9. Ibid.

10. Lopez, Gonzalez-Barrera, and Cuddington, "Diverse Origins: The Nation's 14 Largest Hispanic Origin Groups."

11. Ibid.

12. Ibid.

13. Ibid.

14. Ibid.

15. Sanchez, "Taking a Closer Look at Latino Pan-Ethnic Identity."

16. Ibid.

17. Luis R. Fraga, John A. Garcia, Rodney E. Hero, Michael Jones-Correa, Valerie Marinez-Ebers, and Gary M. Segura, *Latinos in the New Millennium*, (New York: Cambridge University Press, 2012).

18. Taylor, Lopez, Martínez, and Velasco, "When Labels Don't Fit: Hispanics and Their Views of Identity."

19. Ibid.

20. "The Hispanic Influence on American Culture," 2012, Conill, http://conill.com/images/uploads/thinking/The_Hispanic_Influence_on _America.pdf.

21. Ibid.

22. Ibid.

23. Ibid.

24. Ibid.

25. Ibid.

26. Pew Research Center, "Latinos Perceptions of Discrimination," November 2010, www.pewresearch.org/daily-number/latinos-perceptions-of -discrimination.

27. Pew Research Center, Hispanic Trends Project, "Between Two Worlds: How Young Latinos Come of Age in America," December 2009, updated July 2013, www.pewhispanic.org/2009/12/11/between-two-worlds-how -young-latinos-come-of-age-in-america.

28. Lopez, Morin, and Taylor, "Illegal Immigration Backlash Worries, Divides Latinos Pew Research Center, Hispanic Trends Project."

29. Pew Research Center, "Hispanics: Targets of Discrimination," May 2010, www.pewresearch.org/daily-number/hispanics-targets-of-discrimin ation.

30. Irma Silva-Zolezzi, Alfredo Hidalgo-Miranda, Jesus Estrada-Gil, Juan Carlos Fernandez-Lopez, Laura Uribe-Figueroa, Alejandra Contreras,

Eros Balam-Ortiz, Laura del Bosque-Plata, David Velazquez-Fernandez, Cesar Lara, Rodrigo Goya, Enrique Hernandez-Lemus, Carlos Davila, Eduardo Barrientos, Santiago March, and Gerardo Jimenez-Sanchez, "Analysis of Genomic Diversity in Mexican Mestizo Populations to Develop Genomic Medicine in Mexico," *Proceedings of the National Academy of Sciences of the United States of America*, May 2009, www.ncbi.nlm.nih.gov/pmc/articles/PMC2680428.

31. Ibid.

32. Taylor, Lopez, Martínez, and Velasco, "When Labels Don't Fit: Hispanics and Their Views of Identity."

33. Luis R. Fraga et al., *Latinos in the New Millennium*.

34. Ibid.

35. Ibid.

36. Ibid.

37. Ibid.

38. Pew Research, Social and Demographic Trends Project, "Do Blacks and Hispanics Get Along?," January 2008, www.pewsocialtrends.org/2008/01/31/do-blacks-and-hispanics-get-along.

39. Ibid.

40. Luis R. Fraga et al., *Latinos in the New Millennium*.

41. Ibid.

42. John Halpin and Ruy Teixeira, "Latino Attitudes About Women and Society," Center for American Progress, July 2010, www.americanprogress.org/issues/race/report/2010/07/09/8152/latino-attitudes-about-women-and-society.

43. Ibid.

44. Luis R. Fraga et al., *Latinos in the New Millennium*.

45. Ibid.

46. Ibid.

47. Ibid.

48. Ibid.

49. Ibid.

50. Ibid.

51. United States Census Bureau, "Characteristics of Same-Sex Couple Households," American Community Survey, 2012, http://www.census.gov/hhes/samesex/

52. Anjani Chandra, William D. Mosher, Casey Copen, and Catlainn Sionean, "Sexual Behavior, Sexual Attraction, and Sexual Identity in the United States: Data from the 2006–2008 National Survey of Family Growth," Centers for Disease Control and Prevention, National Center for Health Statistics, March 2011, www.cdc.gov/nchs/data/nhsr/nhsr036.pdf.

53. Ibid.

54. Ibid.

55. Ibid.

56. Taylor, Lopez, Martínez, and Velasco, "When Labels Don't Fit: Hispanics and Their View of Identity."

57. Ibid.

58. Mark Hugo Lopez and Danielle Cuddington, "Latinos Changing Views of Same-Sex Marriage," Pew Research Center, June 2013, www.pewre

search.org/fact-tank/2013/06/19/latinos-changing-views-of-same-sex-marriage.

59. Gary J. Gates, "How Many People Are Lesbian, Gay, Bisexual and Transgender?," Williams Institute, University of California, School of Law, April 2011, http://williamsinstitute.law.ucla.edu/wp-content/uploads/Gates-How-Many-People-LGBT-Apr-2011.pdf.

60. Jaime M. Grant, Lisa A. Mottet, and Justin Tanis, "Injustice at Every Turn: a Report of the National Transgender Discrimination Survey," National Gay and Lesbian Task Force and the National Center for Transgender Equality, February 2011, www.thetaskforce.org/downloads/reports/reports/ntds_full.pdf.

61. Ibid.

62. Pew Research, Hispanic Trends Project, "Between Two Worlds: How Young Latinos Come of Age in America," December 2009, updated July 2013, www.pewhispanic.org/2009/12/11/between-two-worlds-how-young-latinos-come-of-age-in-america.

63. Ibid.

64. Ibid.

65. Ibid.

66. Ibid.

67. National Center for Education Statistics, *Fast Facts: Dropout Rates*, 2013, http://nces.ed.gov/FastFacts/display.asp?id=16; The dropout rate reported above is what is known as the "status dropout rate," the percentage of sixteen through twenty-four year olds not enrolled in school and who have not earned a high school degree or GED certificate.

68. Pew Research, Hispanic Trends Project, "Between Two Worlds: How Young Latinos Come of Age in America."

69. Ibid.

70. Ibid.

71. Ibid.